This Field Guide belongs to:

ANiya

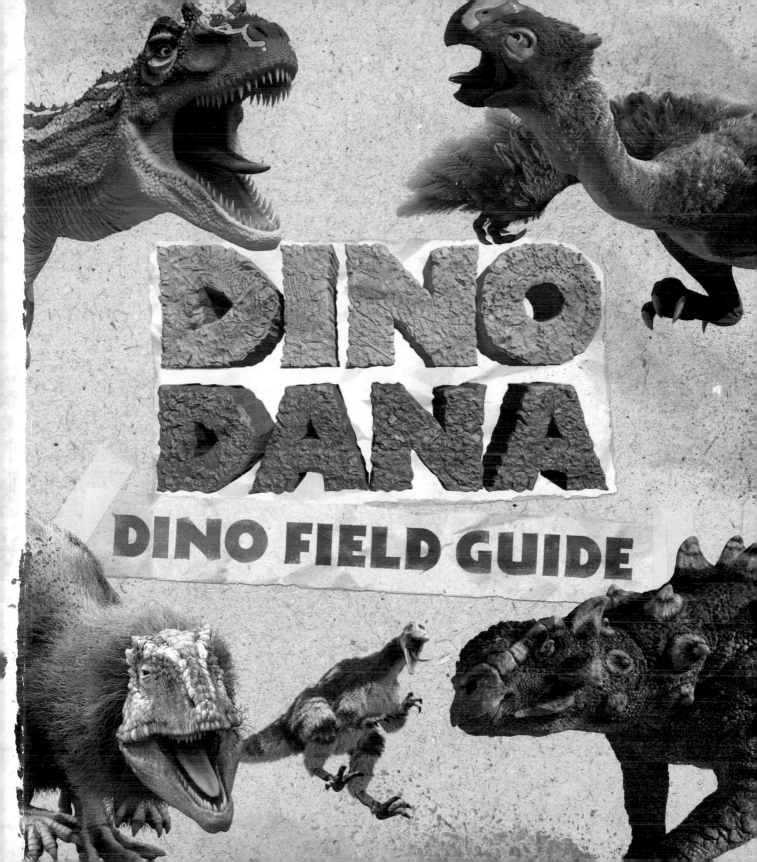

DINO DANA
DINO FIELD GUIDE

That's me!

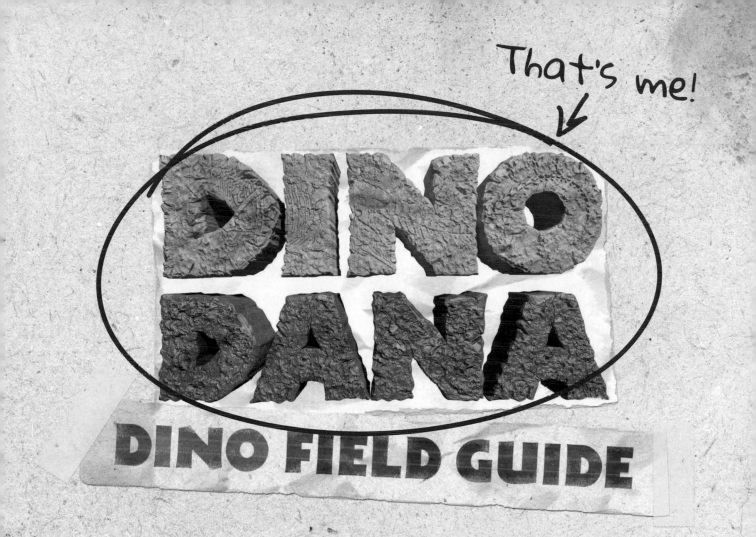

DINO DANA
DINO FIELD GUIDE

J.J. Johnson, Christin Simms &
Colleen Russo Johnson, PhD

mango
PUBLISHING

Coral Gables

Mango is an active supporter of authors' rights to free speech and artistic expression in their books. The purpose of copyright is to encourage authors to produce exceptional works that enrich our culture and our open society.

Uploading or distributing photos, scans or any content from this book without prior permission is theft of the author's intellectual property. Please honor the author's work as you would your own. Thank you in advance for respecting our author's rights.

For permission requests, please contact the publisher at:
Mango Publishing Group
2850 S Douglas Road, 2nd Floor
Coral Gables, FL 33134 USA
info@mango.bz

For special orders, quantity sales, course adoptions and corporate sales, please email the publisher at sales@mango.bz. For trade and wholesale sales, please contact Ingram Publisher Services at customer.service@ingramcontent.com or +1.800.509.4887.

Dino Dana: Dino Field Guide

Library of Congress Cataloging-in-Publication number: 2020933486
ISBN: (p) 978-1-64250-284-8 (e) 978-1-64250-285-5
BISAC category code: JNF003050JUVENILE, NONFICTION / Animals / Dinosaurs & Prehistoric Creatures

Printed in the United States of America

DEDICATION

To Ripley, Rex, and all the kids who live, breathe, and sleep dinosaurs—

Never stop imagining, never stop digging, and never stop seeing the magic in the everyday. There are dinosaurs still waiting to be discovered; go find them!

Love, Dad, Mom, and Aunt Simms

ACKNOWLEDGEMENTS

PALEONTOLOGIST CONSULTANTS

Dr. Victoria Arbour

Dr. David Evans

Dr. Donald Henderson

FOR SINKING SHIP ENTERTAINMENT

Matt Bishop, J.J. Johnson, Blair Powers, Partners

Kate Sanagan and Marilyn Kynaston, Heads of Sales and Distribution

Jason Lean, Book Designer

Special thanks to Alexis Grieve and Nour Mallouh for their endless help.

All dinosaur designs and artwork designed in house by the Sinking Ship Entertainment VFX team.

INTRODUCTION

Hi fellow paleontologist-in-training!

My name is DANA, and this is my FIELD GUIDE. And now your field guide, too!

— people who study dinos

Field guides help paleontologists, like us, to keep notes on all the things we've learned about dinosaurs. AND THERE IS SO MUCH TO LEARN!!!

In fact, we're still learning new things about dinosaurs EVERY DAY.

♥ ♥ LOVE ♥ ♥

One of the reasons I ~~like~~ dinosaurs so much is that we don't know everything about them yet. There's still so much to DISCOVER!

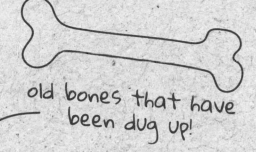

old bones that have been dug up!

Everything we know about dinosaurs comes from studying their fossils and then comparing them to animals that are alive today. After that, it's time for my favourite part: COMING UP WITH A THEORY! ← — a theory is an idea that you get to test.

Inside my field guide, you'll find my notes on a ton of dinosaurs and some of the experiments I've conducted on them. These are my THEORIES based on what I've learned, observed, and imagined.

An experiment lets you test a hypothesis. ← A hypothesis is what you think is going to happen.

EXAMPLE: My hypothesis is that if you like dinosaurs, you're going to LOVE this field guide.

And sometimes our theories or what we thought we knew about a dinosaur are proven wrong. Which is why it's SUPER important to KEEP ASKING QUESTIONS. Otherwise, we'll never learn anything NEW.

* Dinos are like ~~lizards~~. ← more like birds
* Dinos only lived in ~~warm places~~. ← some lived in cold places too
* T. rex arms were ~~weak~~. ← actually strong

There are many, MANY, MAAANNNYYY more experiments to do. Especially as you come up with your very own DINO QUESTIONS.

Why did some dinosaurs have feathers?

What did dinosaurs sound like?

How did dinosaurs get so big?

Paleontologists have found over seven hundred different dinosaurs! Thirty-six of my favorite ones are in this field guide, but there are HUNDREDS, maybe THOUSANDS still waiting to be DUG UP. Maybe by ME and YOU one day!

So let's keep DIGGING for new FACTS, new QUESTIONS, and new DISCOVERIES!

Your fellow paleontologist-in-training,

Dana

HOW TO USE MY FIELD GUIDE

Here are some tips to help you use my field guide for your own dino experiments.

STAMPS!

These make it easy to know which family group each dino belongs to:

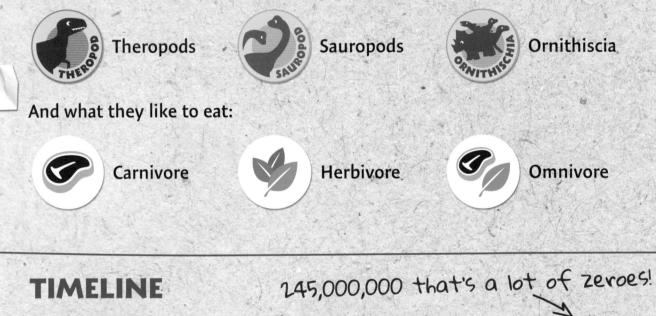

THEROPOD Theropods   **SAUROPOD** Sauropods   **ORNITHISCHIA** Ornithiscia

And what they like to eat:

Carnivore   Herbivore   Omnivore

TIMELINE

245,000,000 that's a lot of zeroes!

This shows you how long ago each dino lived. Dinosaurs lived from 245 to 66 million years ago. And they ruled the earth for over 179 million years.

252 Million   201 Million   145 Million

TRIASSIC   JURASSIC

SIZE CHART!

This shows how big each dinosaur is compared to me.
I'm probably about the same size as you.

Time to start asking some dino questions!
→

Me vs. Troodon

WHERE WE FOUND THEM

This map shows where each dinosaur's fossils
were first discovered.

People have only been around
for a few million years!

| CRETACEOUS | | 66 Million PALEOGENE | 23 Million NEOGENE | 2.6 Million QUATERNARY |

ALBERTOSAURUS

(Al-ber-tuh-sore-us)
Means "Alberta Lizard"

12

⌐252 Million	⌐201 Million	⌐145 Million
TRIASSIC	JURASSIC	

Because the first one was found in what is now Alberta, Canada.

13

WHEN THEY LIVED

US

| CRETACEOUS | | 66 Million | | 23 Million | | 2.6 Million | |
| PALEOGENE | | NEOGENE | | QUATERNARY | | |

ALBERTOSAURUS

14

Has two long powerful legs!

Bipedal, which means it walked on two legs.

★ Was half the size of a T. rex.

★ Weighed as much as 3 moose.

Future Dino Experiment: I wonder how fast they could run?

Face fossils found with bite marks from another Albertosaurus.

OUCH!

mass grave, or bonebed. Paleontologists discovered fossils from over a dozen different Albertosaurus in one place.

Means they could have hunted in packs! Like wolves.

Me vs. Alberto

Why do animals hunt in packs?

1) Take down bigger prey.
2) Safer.
3) Takes less energy.

DINO EXPERIMENT **809**

QUESTION: How do baby Albertosaurus survive?

BACKGROUND RESEARCH NOTES:

This was JUST a dream.
(Dexter didn't REALLY become
a baby Albertosaurus)

Baby Albertosaurus

16

MY PLAN:

Baby Dexter got baby food ALL
OVER my field guide, so I wished
I had a dino brother instead of
Dexter, and my wish came true...
which ended up helping me solve
my dino experiment!

← DEXTER did this!

1. Dexter turned into a baby <u>ALBERTOSAURUS</u> and everyone acted like it was totally normal.

2. The baby dino <u>STOLE</u> my breakfast!! And guess what? Mom just said she was proud of his "dino survival skills."

3. <u>THEN</u> he pushed Saara out of our room and built his dino nest where her bed was. And again, Mom said she was proud of him. Poor Saara.

4. But then he beat me at wrestling, proving he was stronger than <u>ME</u> and I had to move out too!!!

5. The baby Albertosaurus got all of Mom's attention which is what he wanted all along. (I like Dexter better!)

17

FINDING:

<u>Baby dinos compete with their siblings to get food, space, and attention from their parents. The strongest baby dino survives!</u>

AMARGASAURUS

SAUROPOD

(Ah-mar-guh-sore-us)
Means "La Amarga Lizard"

18

WHEN THEY
LIVED

252 Million

TRIASSIC

201 Million

JURASSIC

145 M

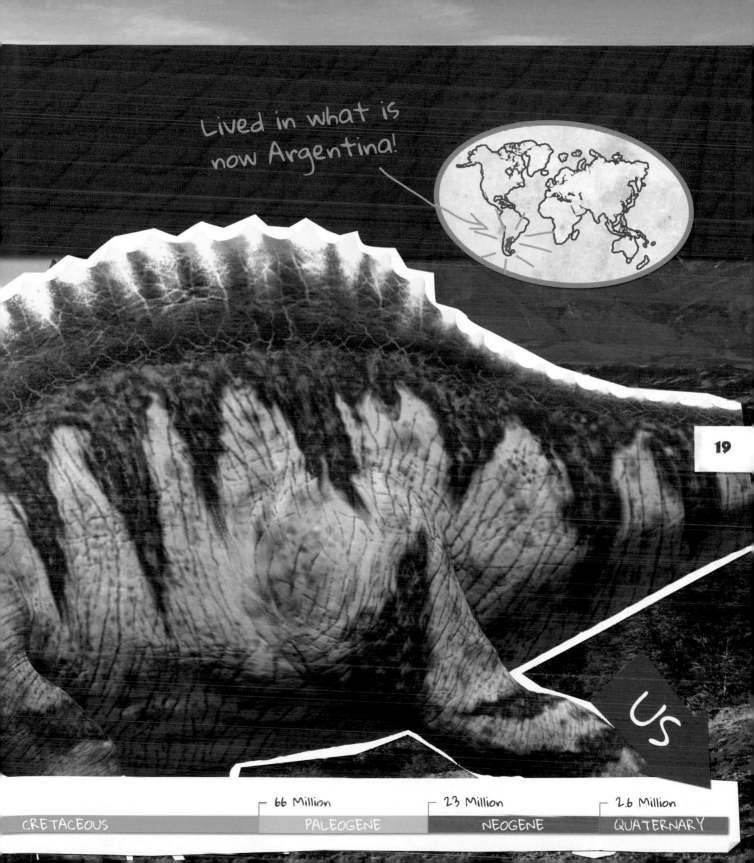

AMARGASAURUS

SPIKES?

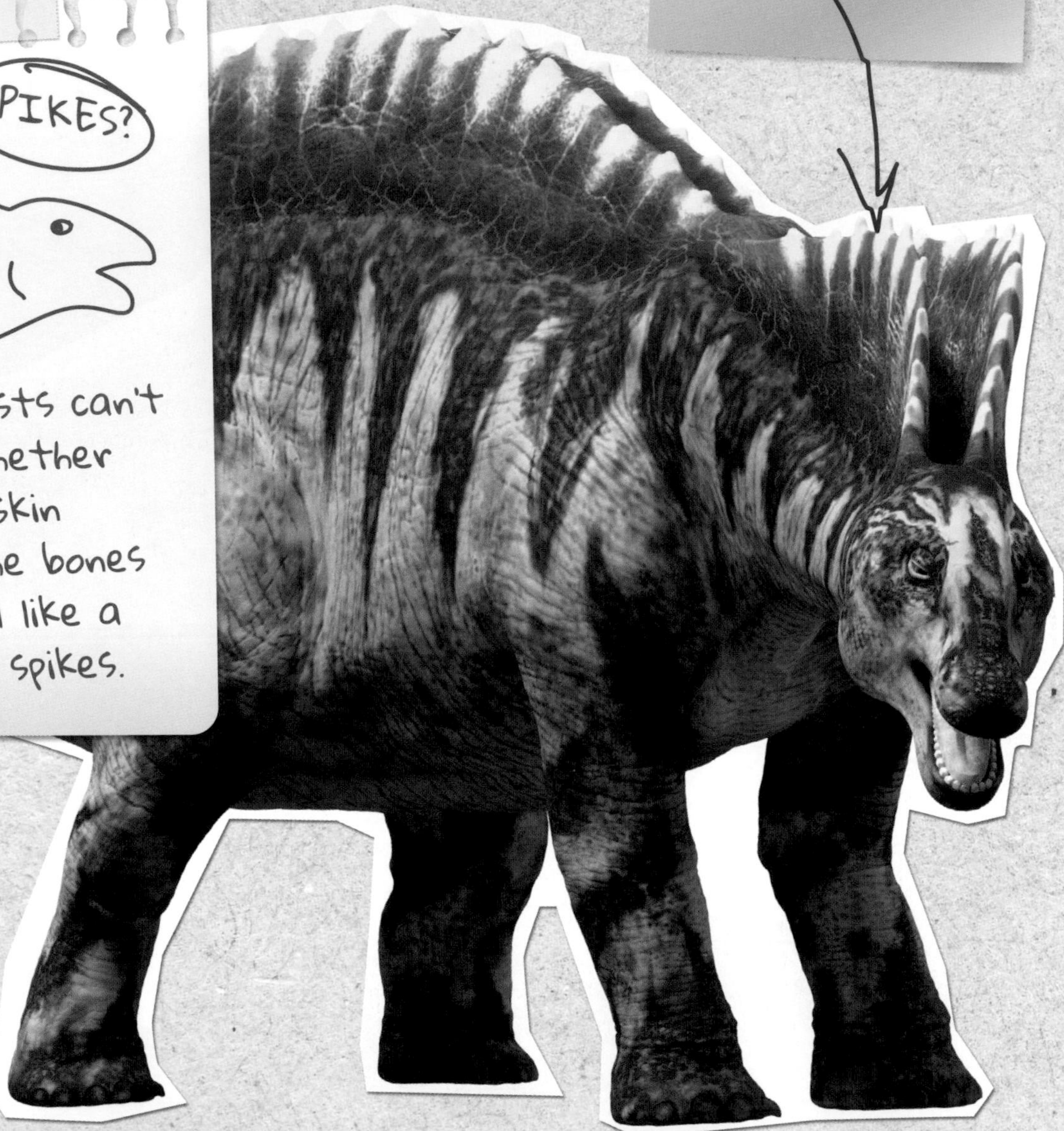

★ Paleontologists can't agree on whether there was skin between the bones that looked like a sail or just spikes.

20

Whatever its neck looked like, they probably used it to show off to other Amargas.

Sauropod means "lizard foot."

Amargasaurus is known from a nearly complete skeleton.

THIS IS A BIG DEAL! Not many sauropods have complete skeletons!

from the growth rings inside fossil bones. Some sauropods lived a long time, up to fifty years or more.

50

Me vs. Amarga

x100!

Weighed more than a hundred jaguars!

QUESTION: Who left the dino poop outside Grandma's barn?!

BACKGROUND RESEARCH NOTES:

Fossilized dino poo is called a COPROLITE.

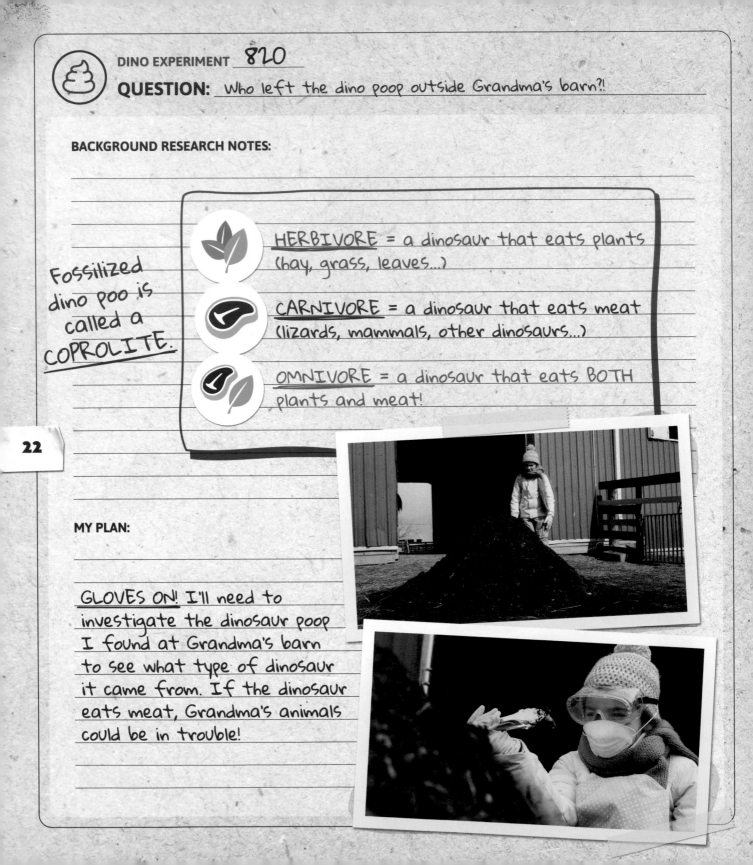

HERBIVORE = a dinosaur that eats plants (hay, grass, leaves...)

CARNIVORE = a dinosaur that eats meat (lizards, mammals, other dinosaurs...)

OMNIVORE = a dinosaur that eats BOTH plants and meat!

22

MY PLAN:

GLOVES ON! I'll need to investigate the dinosaur poop I found at Grandma's barn to see what type of dinosaur it came from. If the dinosaur eats meat, Grandma's animals could be in trouble!

FIELD NOTES:

1. I see hay in the poop, so it must belong to a herbivore. AND I see an Amargasaurus nearby, she must be hanging around to eat the farm animals' hay! ~~Experiment solved!~~

   » Experiment back on! Because there is also a Troodon near the barn! The Troodon eats plants and animals, so I better check the poop again.

2. I found a bone in the poop! Since there is hay AND bone in the poop, it must be from the Troodon! ~~Experiment solved!~~

   » Nope! Because I just saw a T. rex! But the T. rex eats meat, so why would there be hay in its poop?

3. Grandma helped me figure it out! The poop COULD be from the T. rex, because the T. rex ATE dinosaurs that ate hay! Experiment FINALLY solved!

FINDING:

Even though carnivores only ate other animals, their poop could still have plants in it because some of the animals they ate had plants in their stomachs when the carnivore ate them! Isn't that interesting?

BRACHIOSAURUS

SAUROPOD

(Brack-ee-oh-sore-us)
Means "Arm Lizard"

Named the arm lizard because their front legs are longer than their back legs.

WHEN THEY LIVED

252 Million

TRIASSIC

201 Million

end of
JURASSIC

145 Million

Lived in what is now the Western United States.

US

	66 Million	23 Million	2.6 Million
CRETACEOUS	PALEOGENE	NEOGENE	QUATERNARY

BRACHIOSAURUS

Sharp claws on their hind feet could have been used for digging nests for their eggs.

Ate the tops off 18 trees EVERY. SINGLE. DAY!

Their front feet would have made horseshoe-shaped handprints, but their back feet would have left big round footprints.

★ Weighed as much as seven elephants!

Its big size kept it safe from predators.

A <u>predator</u> is an animal that hunts, catches, and eats other animals.

Long necks helped them reach treetops for food, and they had spoon-shaped teeth for eating plants.

Me vs. Brachio

Whoa!

As tall as two giraffes!

One of the tallest known dinosaurs!

DINO EXPERIMENT 624

QUESTION: Why do baby Brachiosaurus eat so much?

BACKGROUND RESEARCH NOTES:

The Brachiosaurus is MASSIVE!
It's a member of the sauropod
family which are really big
herbivores.

Baby Brachiosaurus

MY PLAN:

Observe and brainstorm. Dad is home today and said he would help.

FIELD NOTES:

1. I spotted a baby Brachiosaurus outside but <u>ALL HE DOES</u> is eat, eat, and <u>EAT</u>!
   » Dad hypothesizes it's because the Brachiosaurus needs to become huge! I wonder why it has to be such a big dino?

2. I found a teen Brachy! He's <u>WAY</u> bigger than the baby, but STILL eating!
   » Dad's new hypothesis is that the teen still needs to eat so he can reach his full size to DEFEND himself.
   » Update = A Troodon is here and went after the baby and teen Brachy! The teen defended them by stomping his feet. Bye Troodon!

3. Uh oh! Now a big T. rex is here! She's going after the baby and teen Brachiosaurus! The teen is trying to scare her away, but he's not big enough!
   » Update = A <u>HUGE</u> mama Brachiosaurus came just in time to protect the baby and teen! She stood up on her big two back legs and then <u>STOMPED</u> the ground to scare off the T. rex. It was so loud and so amazing!

FINDING:

The baby Brachiosaurus eats all the time so he can grow to his full size as fast as possible to scare off predators!

COMPSOGNATHUS

(Komp-sog-naw-thus)
Means "Pretty Jaw"

Look how pretty she is!

Lived in in what is now Germany!

WHEN THEY LIVED

┌ 252 Million   ┌ 201 Million   ┌ 145 Million

TRIASSIC   JURASSIC

Theropod means "beast foot."

US

66 Million 23 Million 2.6 Million

CRETACEOUS PALEOGENE NEOGENE QUATLRNARY

COMPSOGNATHUS

* One of the smallest dinosaurs ever discovered.

* Only two sets of fossils have been discovered.

A skeleton was found with a whole lizard in its belly.

Fossil records show that the Compsagnathus had hollow bones like birds.

Which means their bones were strong but not as heavy.

THE TAIL OF THE COMPSOGNATHUS HELPED IT KEEP ITS BALANCE.

Future Dino
Experiment:
Find out how.

33

Ran on two
long, thin legs

Could run as fast
as a dog.

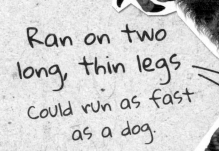

Me vs. Compy

I'm bigger than
a dinosaur!

Only about the
size and weight
of a chicken.

QUESTION: How does the Compsognathus run so fast?

BACKGROUND RESEARCH NOTES:

The Compsognathus uses its small size and speed to outrun predators and steal food!

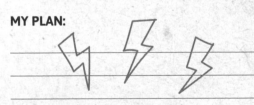

MY PLAN:

I'm going to skateboard down a ramp to go as fast as a Compsognathus! Protective gear ON!

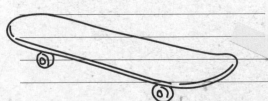

FIELD NOTES:

1. I tried skateboarding down the ramp but it didn't make me fast enough and I also fell...

2. The Compsognathus goes low when he's running fast to avoid other dinosaurs, so I'll try bending down low on my skateboard!
   » Update = Ouch, I fell again!

3. I just noticed that the Compsognathus doesn't <u>JUST</u> go low, he <u>ALSO</u> pushes off with one of his legs to get a burst of speed. I can't wait to try that!!

   » Update = It worked! I went down the ramp and was just as fast as the Compognathus!

FINDING:

The Compsognathus runs super fast by going low <u>AND</u> pushing off with one leg for a burst of speed!... Also, you fall a <u>LOT</u> when you're learning how to skateboard!!!

CORYTHOSAURUS

(Kor-ith-oh-Sore-US)
Means "Helmet Lizard"

ORNITHISCHIA

36

252 Million

201 Million

145 Million

TRIASSIC

JURASSIC

Found in what is now
Alberta, Canada

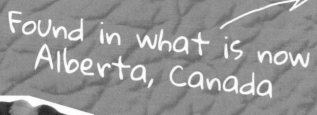

WHEN THEY
LIVED

US

	66 Million	23 Million	2.6 Million
CRETACEOUS	PALEOGENE	NEOGENE	QUATERNARY

CORYTHOSAURUS

Its full name is Corythosaurus casuarius, and the second part means it "looks like a cassowary bird."

Which it kinda did.

★ Lived in herds because it was safer.

★ Beak had no teeth! BUT its jaw had hundreds of teeth and when one wore out another would pop in.

HONK! HONK!

Could send air through the crest on its head to make honking sounds, like a French horn.

Babies were not born with the crest — it started to grow when Corythosaurus were teenagers.

Could walk on two or four legs.

But it was faster on two!

Me vs. Cory

Weighed as much as two cars!

DINO EXPERIMENT 703

QUESTION: Why do Corythosaurus honk?

BACKGROUND RESEARCH NOTES:

Paleontologists believe Corythosaurus could make HUGE honking noises using the big crests at the top of their heads! SO COOL!

40

MY PLAN:

Observe the Corythosaurus to see WHEN and WHY they HONK!

I accidentally started this experiment during Dexter's nap. Oops.

FIELD NOTES:

1. I found a honking Corythosaurus trying to get our groceries out of the car! Another Cory came to help her get into the car, so I gave them some lettuce to make them stop.

2. More honking! This time the Corythosaurus is honking at her sleeping friend because a hungry Giganotosaurus is coming! Luckily, the sleeping Cory woke up and they ran away.

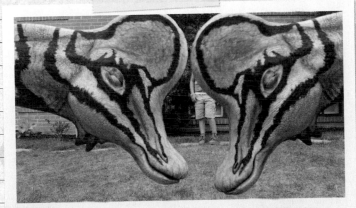

3. Now two Corythosaurus are honking in each other's faces! Wait, I think Mom's calling me...

   » Uh oh. Mom is mad my experiment woke up Dexter, BUT she did tell me that animals make loud noises to show who is the strongest!

   » I know! I'll get them to stop honking by showing them I'M the loudest honker!

FINDING:

Corythosaurus honk for three reasons:

1. To tell each other they found food.
2. To warn each other about predators.
3. To prove who is the strongest.

41

DIABLOCERATOPS

(Dee-ab-low-seh-rah-tops)
Means "Devil Horned Face"

Ornithischia means bird hipped.

Only two diablos have been found so far, in what is now Utah, USA

252 Million   201 Million   145 Million

TRIASSIC   JURASSIC

43

WHEN THEY LIVED

US

CRETACEOUS		66 Million	23 Million	2.6 Million
		PALEOGENE	NEOGENE	QUATERNARY

★ Weighed about as much as six elk.

44

Had teeth for chopping instead of grinding.

Got its name from the curved horns at the back of their frill.

Very small nose horn!

Used its parrot-like beak to rip leaves off branches.

Related to the Triceratops but is much smaller.

Me vs. Diablo

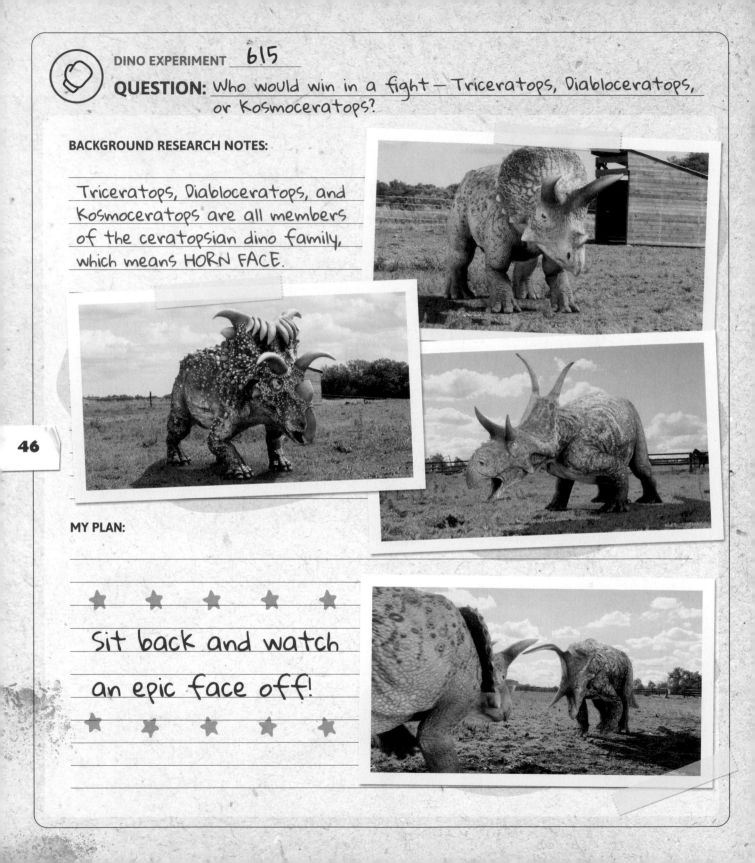

DINO EXPERIMENT __615__

QUESTION: Who would win in a fight — Triceratops, Diabloceratops, or Kosmoceratops?

BACKGROUND RESEARCH NOTES:

Triceratops, Diabloceratops, and Kosmoceratops are all members of the ceratopsian dino family, which means HORN FACE.

MY PLAN:

★ ★ ★ ★ ★

Sit back and watch an epic face off!

★ ★ ★ ★ ★

FIELD NOTES:

<u>HYPOTHESIS:</u> Grandma, Saara, and I all have different hypotheses of who we think will win!

★ Grandma predicts the Kosmoceratops will win because she has the most horns.

★ Saara predicts that the Triceratops will win because she is the biggest of the three dinos.

★ And I predict the Diabloceratops will win because she has the longest horns.

1. <u>ROUND ONE:</u> Triceratops vs. Diabloceratops.
   The Triceratops is larger but the Diabloceratops made herself look bigger by showing off her long horns and scaring the Triceratops.
   ≫ Winner = <u>DIABLOCERATOPS!</u>

2. <u>ROUND TWO:</u> Diabloceratops vs. Kosmoceratops.
   The Kosmoceratops uses all her horns to fight, but the Diablo uses her LONGER horns to push the Kosmo back!
   ≫ Winner = <u>DIABLOCERATOPS!</u>
   (And also me because my prediction was right!)

FINDING:

The long horns of the Diabloceratops make her extremely powerful!

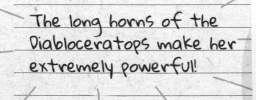

DIPLODOCUS

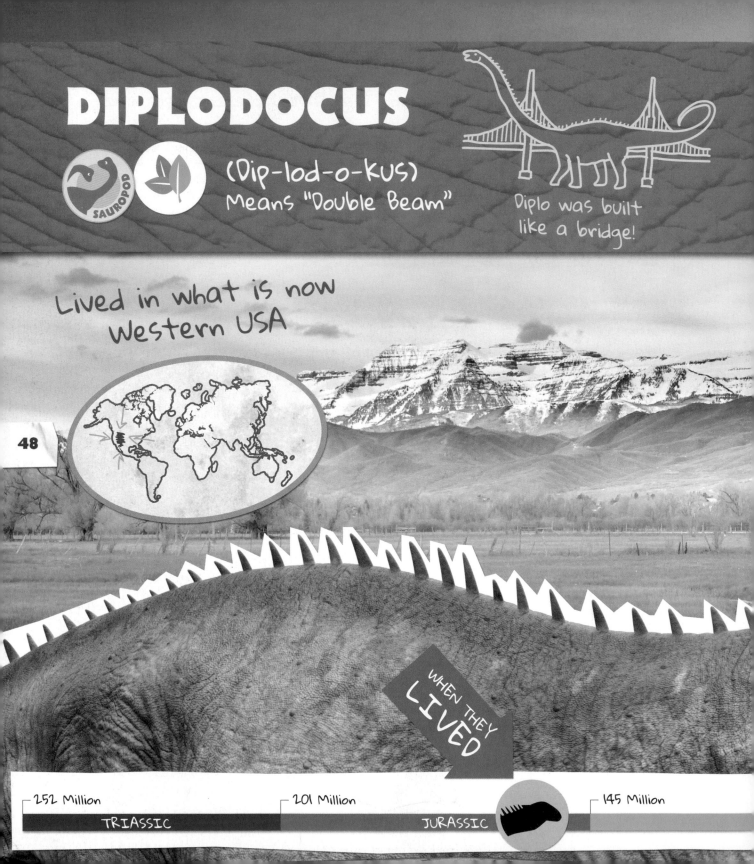

SAUROPOD

(Dip-lod-o-kus)
Means "Double Beam"

Diplo was built like a bridge!

Lived in what is now Western USA

48

WHEN THEY LIVED

252 Million	201 Million	145 Million
TRIASSIC	JURASSIC	

US

66 Million	23 Million	2.6 Million
CRETACEOUS	PALEOGENE	NEOGENE	QUATERNARY

DIPLODOCUS

One of the longest dinosaurs EVER discovered.

CRACK!

Used its tail to make a whipping sound to scare off predators!

* Almost as long as a jumbo jet!

* Huge body but tiny head.

Thigh bone was as long as my mom!

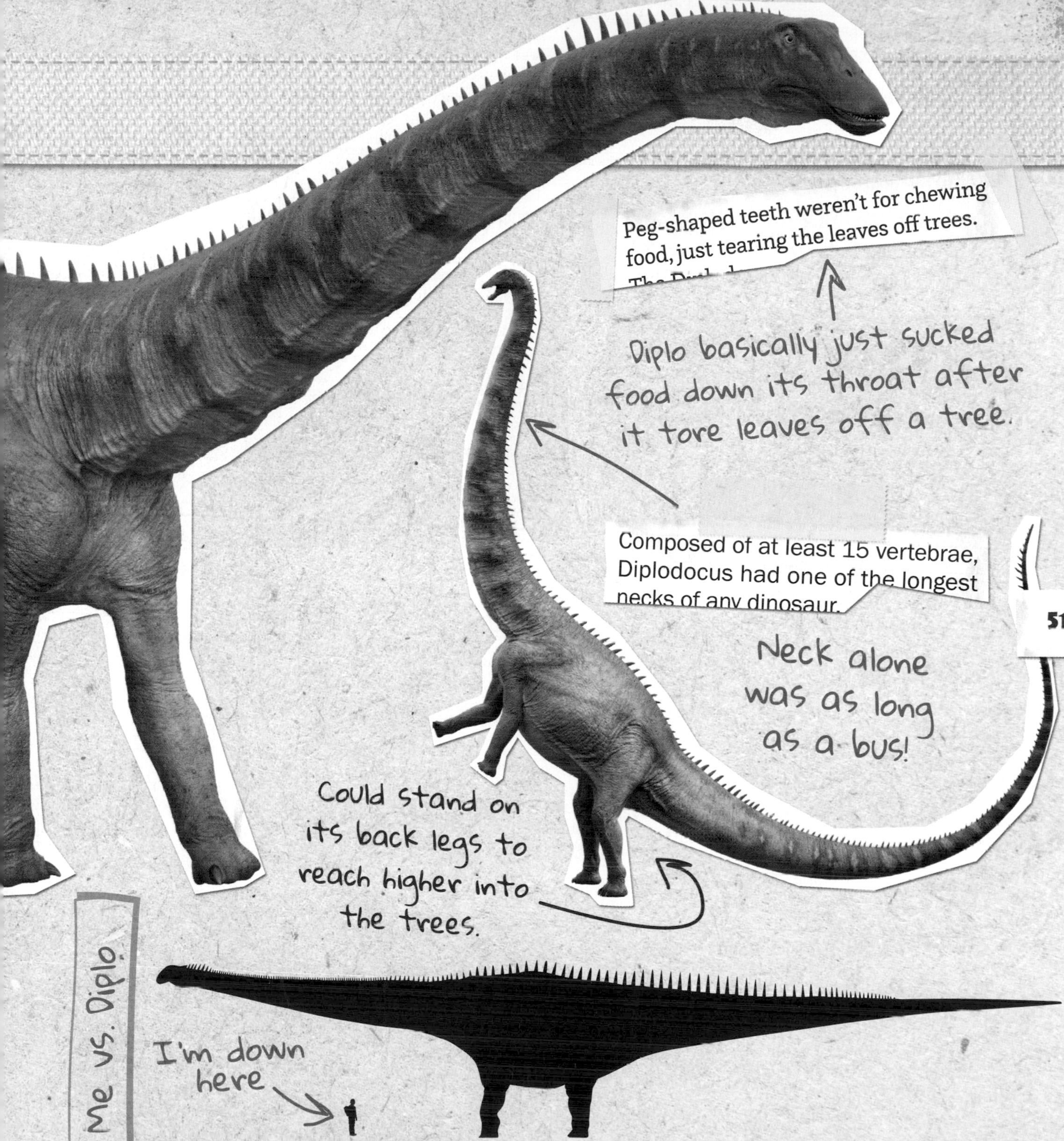

Peg-shaped teeth weren't for chewing food, just tearing the leaves off trees.
~~The Dip~~

Diplo basically just sucked food down its throat after it tore leaves off a tree.

Composed of at least 15 vertebrae, Diplodocus had one of the longest necks of any dinosaur.

Neck alone was as long as a bus!

Could stand on its back legs to reach higher into the trees.

Me vs. Diplo

I'm down here

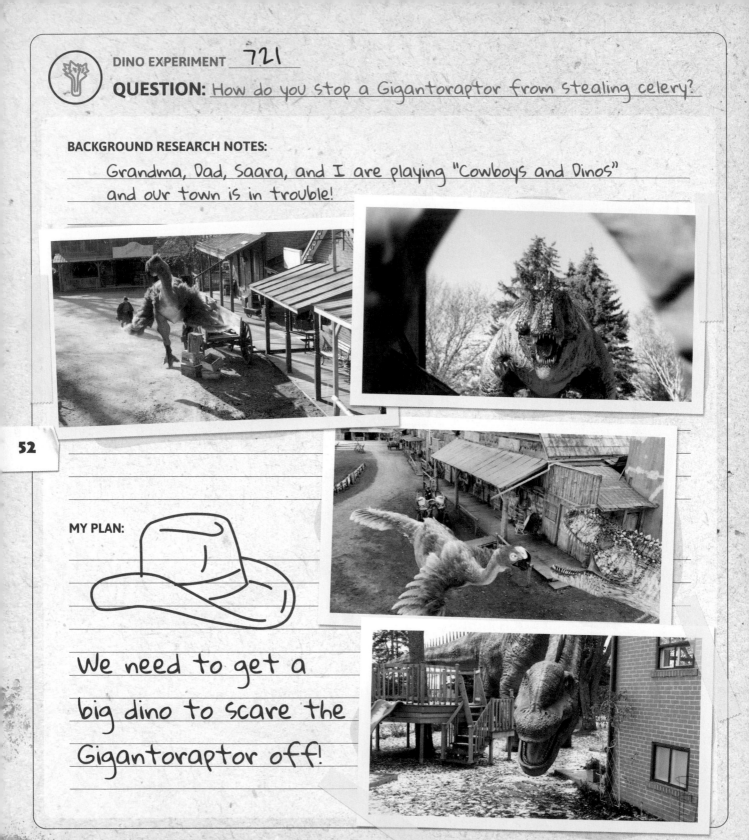

DINO EXPERIMENT ___721___

QUESTION: How do you stop a Gigantoraptor from stealing celery?

BACKGROUND RESEARCH NOTES:

Grandma, Dad, Saara, and I are playing "Cowboys and Dinos" and our town is in trouble!

MY PLAN:

We need to get a big dino to scare the Gigantoraptor off!

FIELD NOTES:

1. The Gigantoraptor is eating all of the celery in our Western town!!

2. The huge Giganotosaurus comes to town to scare off the Gigantoraptor!
   » Update = It worked! Now the celery will be safe... but NOW we have to get rid of a hungry Giga who eats horses and...PEOPLE! We need an even bigger dino who can scare him off!

3. Enter the Diplodocus, one of the longest herbivores of all time. She can whip her huge tail at the Giganotosaurus to scare him off! And not eat us!

   » Update = It worked! The town is safe!

FINDING:

The Diplodocus uses her tail as a large whip to scare off predators!

55

WHEN THEY
LIVED

US

CRETACEOUS		66 Million		23 Million		2.6 Million
		PALEOGENE		NEOGENE		QUATERNARY

DRACOREX

★ Draco's full name is Dracorex hogwartsia which means "the Dragon King of Hogwarts."

★ Was named after the Wizarding School Hogwarts in the Harry Potter books.

Dracorex was three wands high and two brooms long.

Has lots of small spikes all over the back of its head.

The current theory is that it may not be its own dinosaur at all. Paleontologists think it might just be a younger Pachycephalosaurus before it grew the dome on its head.

Paleontologists also think the Stygimoloch was a TEEN version of the Pachycephalosaurus!

Me vs. Draco

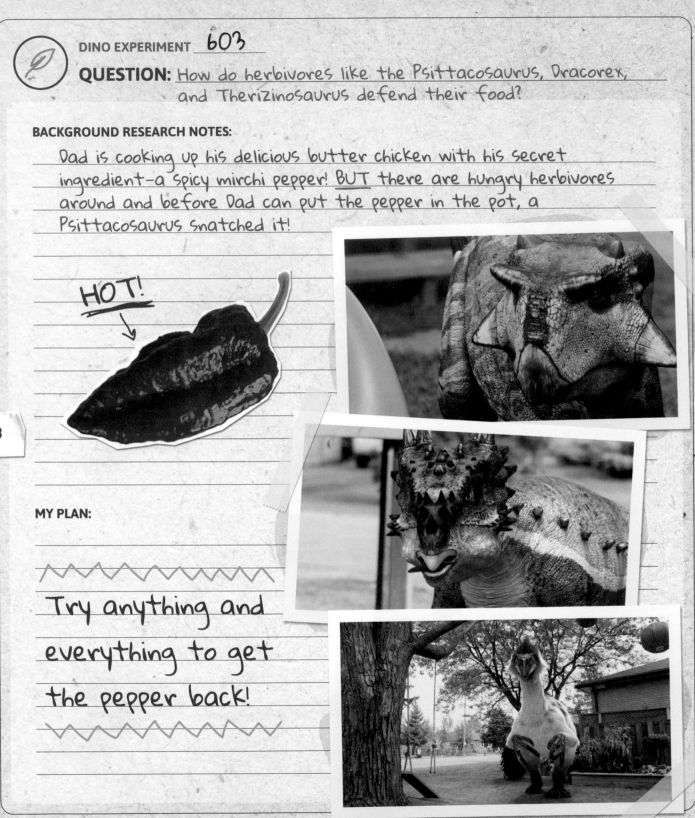

DINO EXPERIMENT __603__

QUESTION: How do herbivores like the Psittacosaurus, Dracorex, and Therizinosaurus defend their food?

BACKGROUND RESEARCH NOTES:

Dad is cooking up his delicious butter chicken with his secret ingredient—a spicy mirchi pepper! BUT there are hungry herbivores around and before Dad can put the pepper in the pot, a Psittacosaurus snatched it!

HOT!

MY PLAN:

Try anything and everything to get the pepper back!

FIELD NOTES:

1. I'm following the Psittacosaurus and I think he's using his quills to protect the pepper!
   » Update = I was able to get it back by running ahead and outsmarting him!

2. But now a Dracorex has stolen the pepper!
   » Update = I became a Dracorex to challenge her to a duel. The Dracorex used her spiky head to try to headbutt me, but I moved out of the way so she slammed into a tree and dropped the pepper! Phew!

3. Uh oh...now a Therizinosaurus has the pepper in his claws! He won't let go!
   » Update = The Therizinosaurus ate the spicy pepper but hated it and spit it out right into Dad's pot of butter chicken! I got the pepper back... Well, most of it! Sorry Dad!

FINDING:

1. The Psittacosaurus may use his quills for defense.
2. The Dracorex uses her head full of horns and spikes to headbutt.
3. The Therizinosaurus uses his super-long claws to defend himself and his food.

DROMAEOSAURUS

(Droh-mee-uh-Sore-US)
Means "Running Lizard"

60

Fossils located in what is now Alberta, Canada

252 Million
201 Million
145 Million
TRIASSIC
JURASSIC

Could run almost as fast as a horse!

WHEN THEY LIVED

US

CRETACEOUS | 66 Million | 23 Million | 2.6 Million
PALEOGENE | NEOGENE | QUATERNARY

DROMAEOSAURUS

Big eyes, excellent vision.

Great sense of smell.

★ Weighed as much as two red foxes!

62

Sickle.

Had a sickle-shaped claw on each foot.

Had a LARGE brain. One of the smartest dinosaurs, but was it the _smartest_?

Possible Dino Experiment!

How did it attack?

Probably pounced on prey and used its claws to pin them down.

Prey is an animal that's hunted by another animal.

Retractable claws. Like a cat.

Me vs. Dromy

63

DINO EXPERIMENT ___617___

QUESTION: Why is the Dromaeosaurus sticking meat on the bushes?

BACKGROUND RESEARCH NOTES:

★ Birds came from Dinosaurs!

★ Female Dromaeosaurus are bigger than male Dromaeosaurus!

64

MY PLAN:

Observe a Dromaeosaurus by using my backpack to BECOME a Dromy.

FIELD NOTES:

1. Today I'm a Dromaeosaurus, and another Dromaeosaurus keeps sticking meat on the bushes and then looking at me. Fascinating.

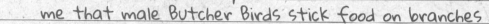

   » Update = I told Mom and Dad about it, and they told me that male Butcher Birds stick food on branches to impress female Butcher Birds!

   » Since birds came from dinosaurs, does that mean the male Dromaeosaurus is trying to impress... ME?

2. Now there are a bunch of Compsognathus eating the meat off the bushes!

   » Update = The male Dromaeosaurus chased off all the Compys and then gave me a shiny ROCK!! He must really want to impress me!!!

   » Update again = An actual female Dromaeosaurus came along and the male Dromaeosaurus gave the pretty shiny rock to her instead. Ouch. But I guess they're a better match...

FINDING:

Just like Butcher Birds, Dromys try to impress each other!

65

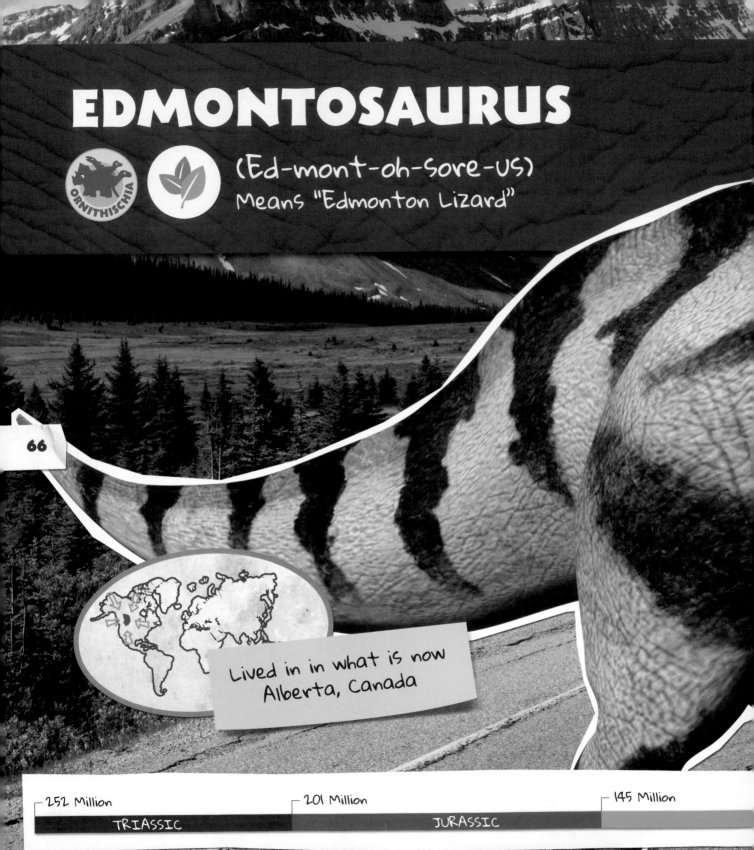

EDMONTOSAURUS

(Ed-mont-oh-sore-us)
Means "Edmonton Lizard"

ORNITHISCHIA

66

Lived in in what is now
Alberta, Canada

252 Million	201 Million	145 Million
TRIASSIC	JURASSIC	

WHEN THEY LIVED

US

CRETACEOUS		66 Million	23 Million	2.6 Million
		PALEOGENE	NEOGENE	QUATERNARY

EDMONTOSAURUS

Shovel-like beak at the front of the mouth.

68

★ There have been more Edmontosaurus bones found than any other dinosaur!

★ Called the 'Cow of the Cretaceous' because we've found so many of them.

MOO!

Was as long as five and a half cows and as heavy as 20 cows!

Over a thousand teeth in the upper and lower jaws combined, but not all were being used to grind food. Some were backup for when the others wore down from too much eating.

It's like when your baby teeth fall out, but Edmontosaurus had more than one backup.

No special horns or weapons on its body to defend itself, but living in herds helped protect Edmontosaurus from predators like the Albertosaurus.

Me vs. Edmonto

Edmontosaurus and Albertosaurus lived in the same area at the same time!

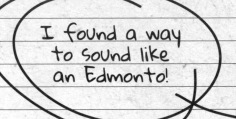

DINO EXPERIMENT __521__

QUESTION: How did the Edmontosaurus defend themselves?

BACKGROUND RESEARCH NOTES:

The Edmontosaurus didn't have any defenses on their bodies (no horns, no spikes, no hard shell!).

I found a way to sound like an Edmonto!

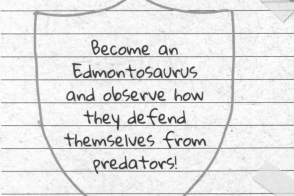

MY PLAN:

Become an Edmontosaurus and observe how they defend themselves from predators!

FIELD NOTES:

1. I'm in Edmontosaurus mode, and to attract an Edmontosaurus family I'm blowing my horn! Mooo!
   » Update = They came BUT they also chewed up my horn!!

2. And now I see why... My loud horn attracted a Giganotosaurus! Oops.
   » Update = The Edmontosaurus made quiet noises to warn each other about the Giga and then quietly ran away!

3. Oh no! The Giganotosaurus spotted them!
   » Update = They made loud mooing sounds to try and scare the Giga off, but it's not working!

4. Now they're running away on their two hind legs as fast as they can!

FINDING:

Ways Edmontosaurus defend themselves:

★ Stay quiet and hide so they don't attract predators.
★ Warn each other when predators show up.
★ Make loud noises to scare off predators.
★ Run away on their two hind legs as fast as possible.

Paleontologists now think that only kid and teen Edmontos could run on their hind legs, adults weigh too much!

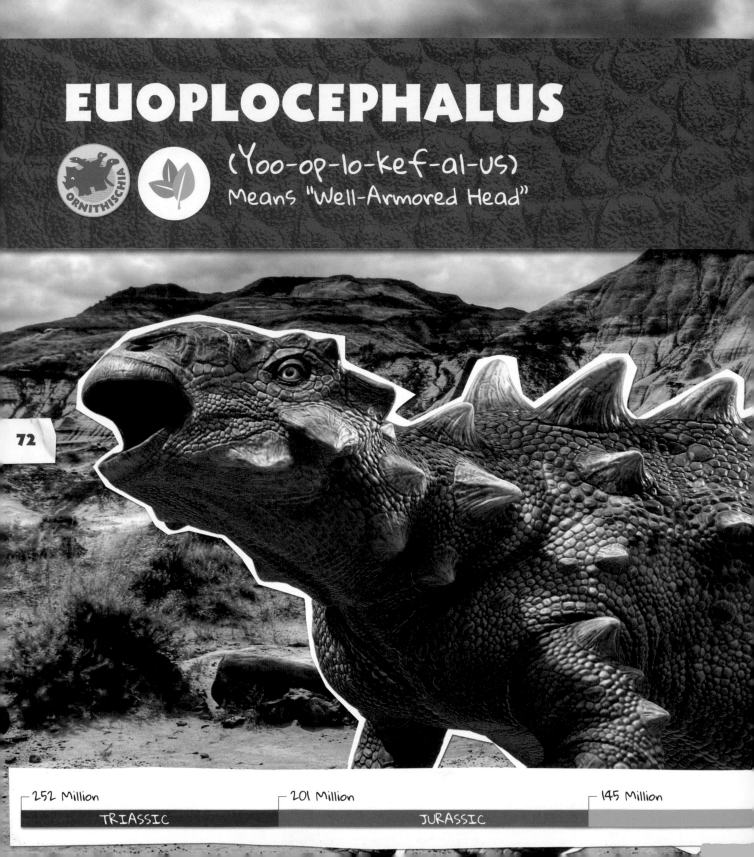

EUOPLOCEPHALUS

ORNITHISCHIA

(Yoo-op-lo-kef-al-us)
Means "Well-Armored Head"

72

252 Million

201 Million

145 Million

TRIASSIC

JURASSIC

Lived in what what is now Alberta, Canada

WHEN THEY LIVED

US

| CRETACEOUS | | 66 Million PALEOGENE | 23 Million NEOGENE | 2.6 Million QUATERNARY |

EUOPLOCEPHALUS

Swung its tail at predators like a baseball bat.

★ The armor plates were bones that grow in the skin, like an armadillo's armor.

It had a heavy tail club that it used for defense. The tail was stiff at the end and had a huge blob of bone at the tip, like a sledgehammer.

Could easily smash bones with a strike from its tail club.

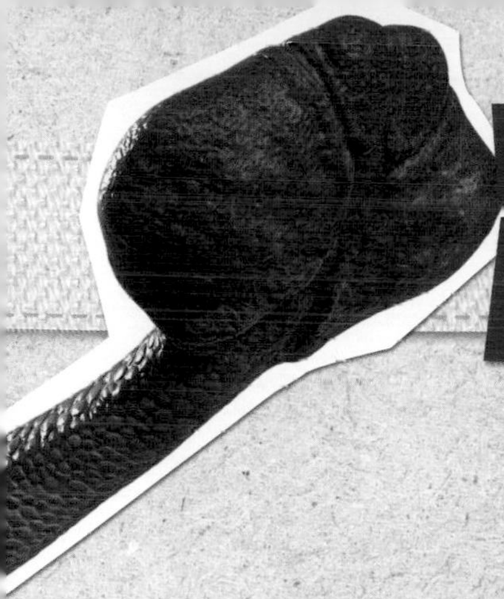

COVERED IN THICK ARMOR SO WAS HEAVY AND SLOW MOVING.

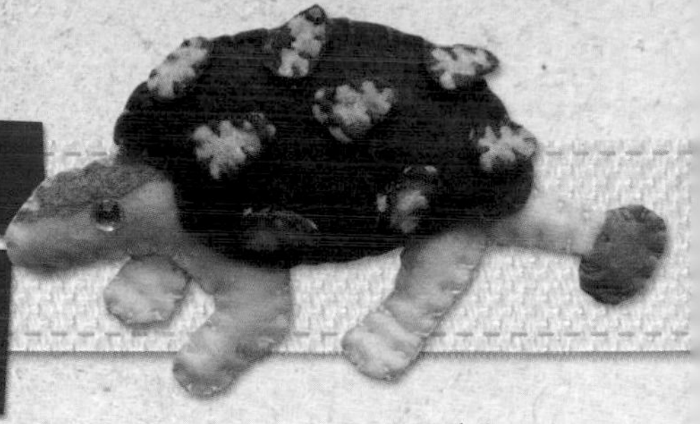

Armor on the neck was like a spiked dog collar.

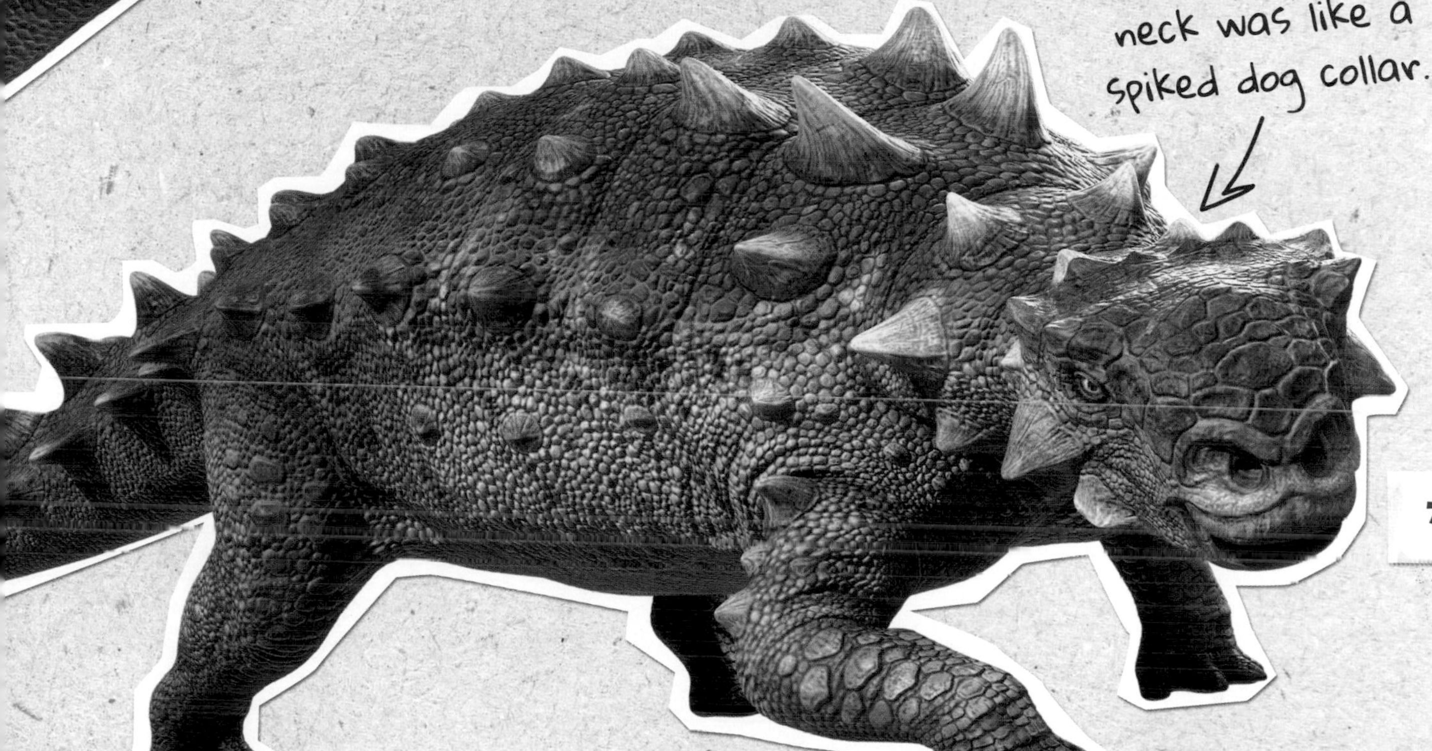

For something so big, its teeth were really small, only as big as one of my fingernails.

Very large dinosaur with a wide body built like a tank!

Me vs. Euoplocephalus

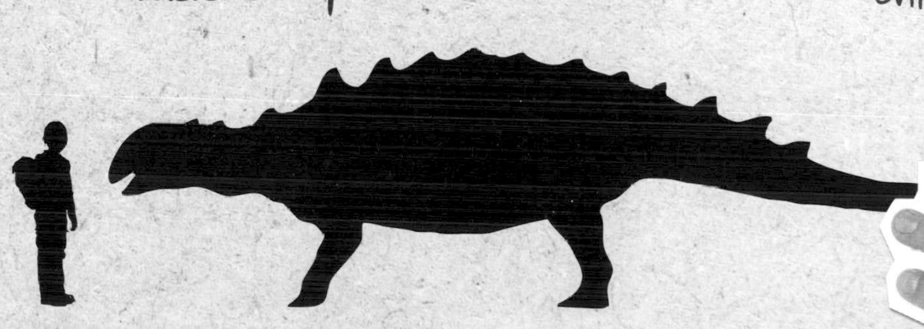

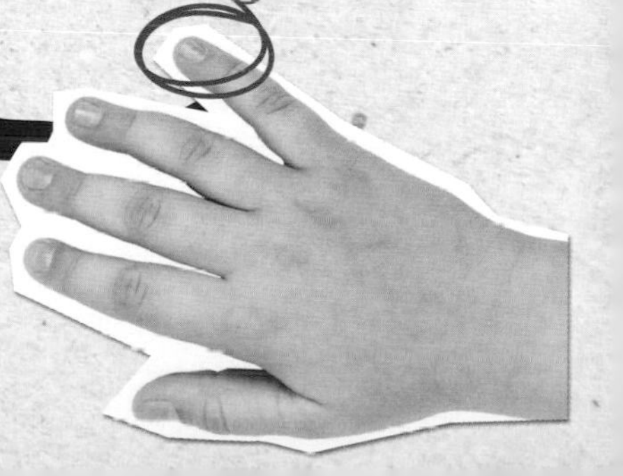

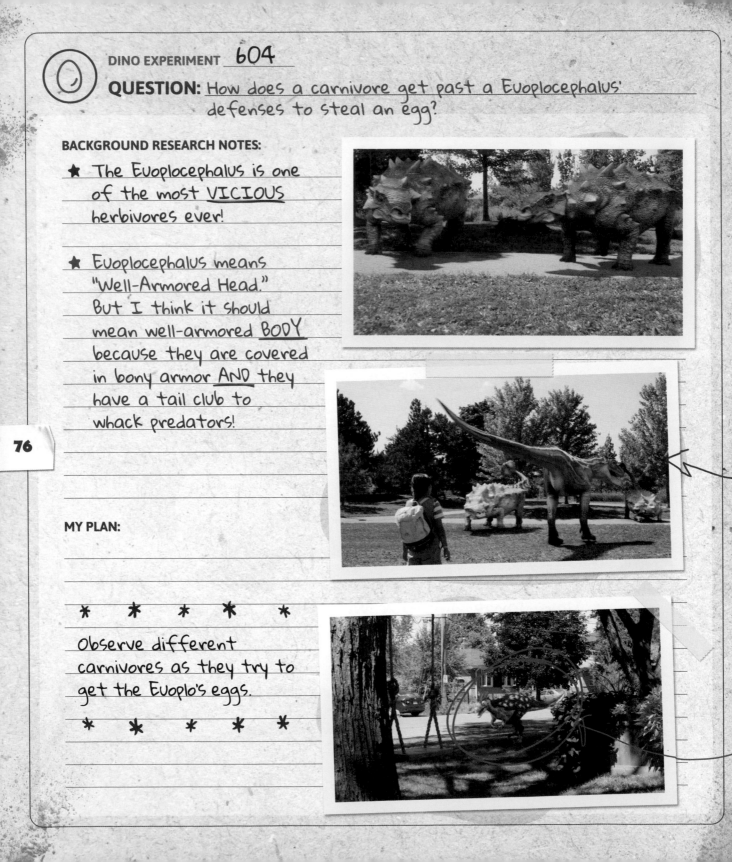

QUESTION: How does a carnivore get past a Euoplocephalus' defenses to steal an egg?

BACKGROUND RESEARCH NOTES:

★ The Euoplocephalus is one of the most UNDERLINED VICIOUS herbivores ever!

★ Euoplocephalus means "Well-Armored Head." But I think it should mean well-armored BODY because they are covered in bony armor AND they have a tail club to whack predators!

76

MY PLAN:

* * * * *

Observe different carnivores as they try to get the Euoplo's eggs.

* * * * *

FIELD NOTES:

1. First up—a powerful Albertosaurus with dozens of sharp teeth.
   » Update = The Euoplocephalus knocked the Albertosaurus over with her tail club!
   » Winner = Euoplocephalus!

2. Next up—a speedy Dromaeosaurus
   » Update = The Dromaeosaurus sped past the tail club but can't make it past the Euplo's body armour!!
   » Winner = Euoplocephalus!

3. Finally—a tiny Microraptor
   » Update = The Microraptor is so small she was able to glide right past the tail and underneath the body armour to steal an egg!!
   » Winner = Microraptor!

FINDING:

- -

To get past a heavily armored dinosaur like the Euoplocephalus being SMALL and SNEAKY like the Microraptor is best!

- -

EUROPASAURUS

(Yoo-rope-ah-sore-us)
Means "Europe Lizard"

SAUROPOD

WHEN THEY LIVED

252 Million	201 Million		145 Million
TRIASSIC		JURASSIC	

Lived in what is now Germany

US

CRETACEOUS	PALEOGENE	NEOGENE	QUATERNARY
	66 Million	23 Million	2.6 Million

* Most sauropods were huge but Euraposaurus was tiny.

★ One Brachiosaurus weighed as much as **30** Europosaurus!

80

(Why didn't it get big?)

Probably lived on a tiny island, so:

↓

• Not a lot of food.

• Not a lot of space.

• Not a lot of predators so didn't need to grow big for defense.

Was only as long as half a school bus.

Me vs. Euoplocephalus

DINO EXPERIMENT 724

QUESTION: Why was the Europasaurus so small?

BACKGROUND RESEARCH NOTES:

★ The Europasaurus is the smallest member of the sauropod family which has a lot of huge dinosaurs!

★ Paleontologists think the Europasaurus lived on a little island that did not have a lot of food or predators.

MY PLAN:

I'm stuck cleaning my room today, so I have no idea how I'm going to solve this dino experiment!

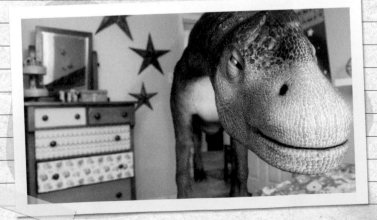

82

FIELD NOTES:

1. I see a Europasaurus outside! Maybe I can get him to come to my window with some lettuce!

   » Update = It didn't come back to my window, it came IN MY ROOM! I repeat, there is a Europasaurus IN. MY. ROOM!

   » Update = The Europasaurus ate all the lettuce and now we're stuck with no more food... kind of like the Europasaurus was stuck on an island!

2. Other Sauropods got big because they HAD to grow huge to defend themselves from predators, BUT maybe the Europasaurus didn't have to because there weren't a lot of predators where they lived....

FINDING:

The Europasaurus was small because he didn't NEED to get large to defend itself from predators and COULDN'T get big because there wasn't enough food on their island to make them big!

FUTALOGNKOSAURUS

SAUROPOD

(Foo-teh-long-ko-sore-us)
Means "Giant Chief Lizard"

252 Million	201 Million	145 Million
TRIASSIC	JURASSIC	

Lived in what is now Argentina!

WHEN THEY LIVED

US

| CRETACEOU | 66 Million PALEOGENE | 23 Million NEOGENE | 2.6 Million QUATERNARY |

FUTALOGNKOSAURUS

Neck was as long as five of my Dads.

★ Weighed more than 8 elephants!

One of the biggest dinosaurs ever discovered!

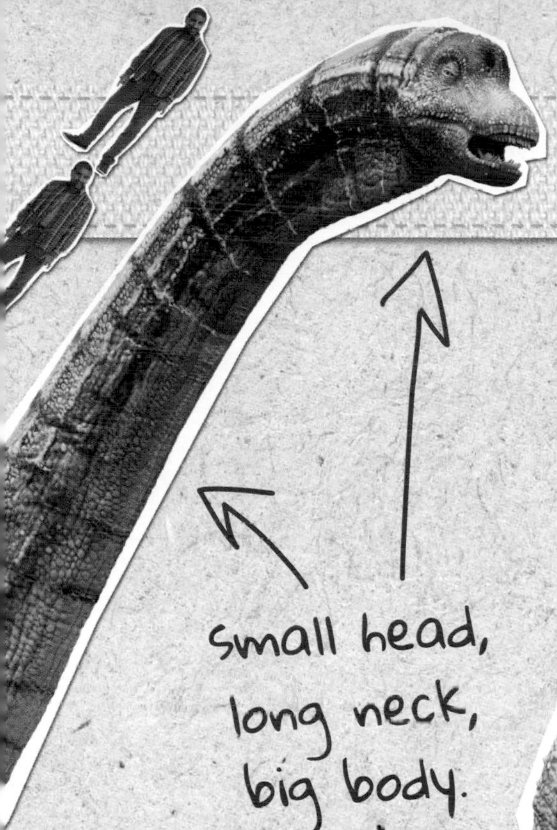

Small head, long neck, big body.

It took five years to dig up the skeleton.

That's half my age!!

Nests had 15 to 40 ostrich sized eggs in them.

Me vs. Futa.

WOW!

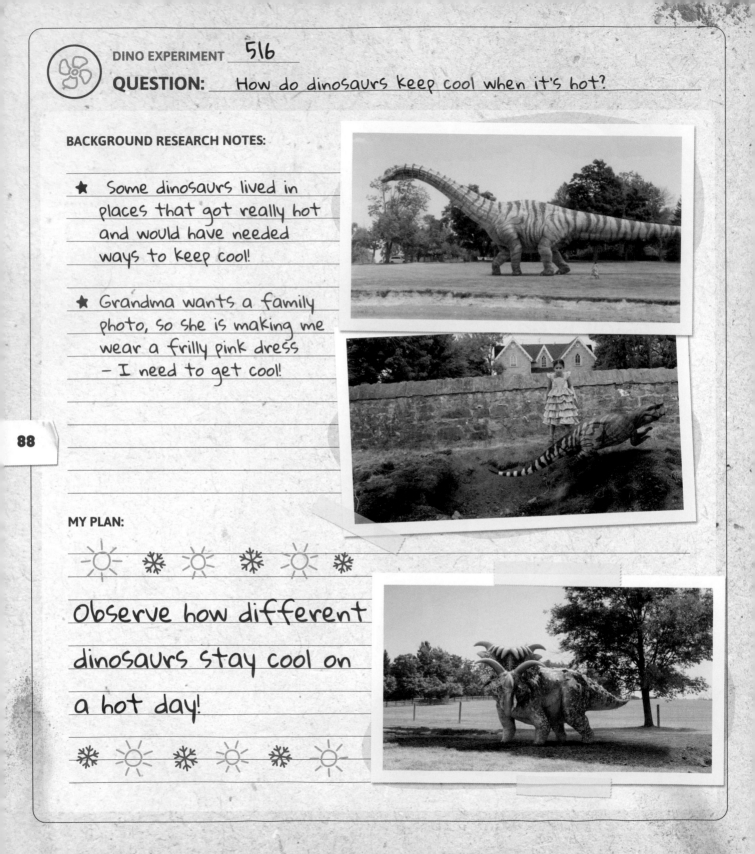

DINO EXPERIMENT 516

QUESTION: How do dinosaurs keep cool when it's hot?

BACKGROUND RESEARCH NOTES:

★ Some dinosaurs lived in places that got really hot and would have needed ways to keep cool!

★ Grandma wants a family photo, so she is making me wear a frilly pink dress — I need to get cool!

MY PLAN:

Observe how different dinosaurs stay cool on a hot day!

FIELD NOTES:

1. I see a Futalognkosaurus hiding under a tree to block the sun. It is cooler in the shade of the tree, but she's so huge the tree only covers part of her massive body! Poor big Futa.

2. The Psittacosaurus is digging a hole. To investigate, I got into the hole and found out it's cooler inside. Smart move to stay out of the sun, Psitta!

3. There's a Kosmoceratops rolling around in MUD and he splashed mud all over ME. Now I'm really dirty but also...much cooler! The mud must help keep the sun off his skin to stay cool. (Like dino sunblock!)

FINDING:

Dinosaurs had lots of ways they kept cool!

★ Found shade under trees.
★ Dug holes to make their own shade.
★ Covered themselves in mud to help keep the sun off their bodies.

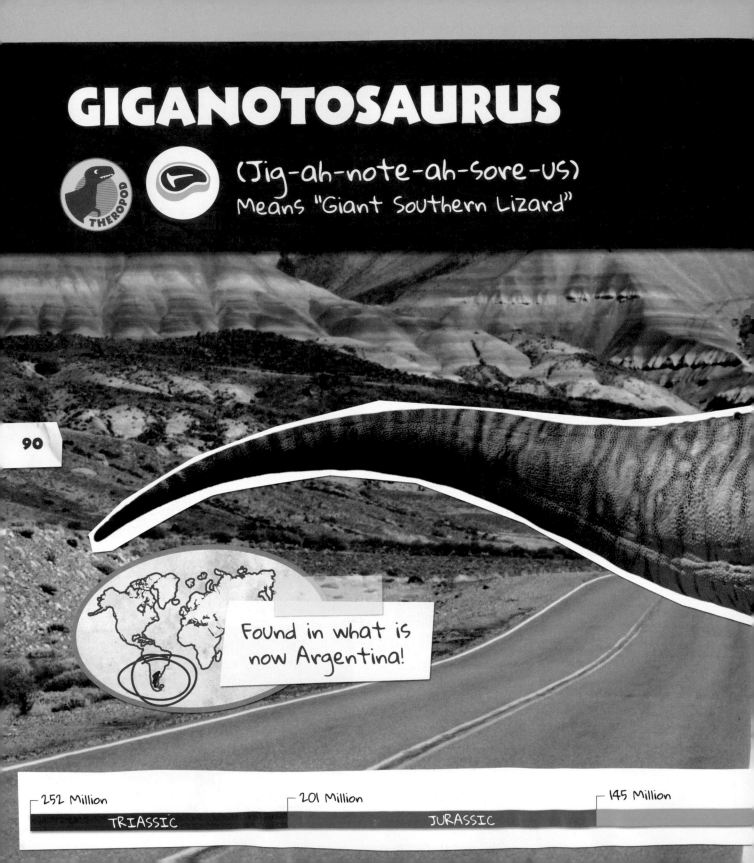

GIGANOTOSAURUS

THEROPOD

(Jig-ah-note-ah-sore-us)
Means "Giant Southern Lizard"

Found in what is now Argentina!

252 Million

201 Million

145 Million

TRIASSIC

JURASSIC

WHEN GIGA LIVED

US

66 Million
PALEOGENE

23 Million
NEOGENE

2.6 Million
QUATERNARY

CRE

GIGANOTOSAURUS

★ One of the biggest meat-eating dinosaurs ever discovered.

★ Even bigger than T. rex!

Giganotasaurus was a member of the carcharodontosaurid family which means "shark toothed lizard." Other members of this family included Allo-

Should mean "shark toothed birds" because dinosaurs were more like birds than lizards.

Brain was only as big as a banana.

Had blade-like teeth.

Not good for crunching, better at slashing and cutting.

Probably ate sauropod dinosaurs.

T. rex was the apex predator in North America.

Giganotosaurus was the apex predator in South America.

Me vs. Giga

Snack sized!

Apex predator means that nothing else can eat it.

QUESTION: Who would win in the fight, the Giganotosaurus or the T. rex?

BACKGROUND RESEARCH NOTES:

★ Some paleontologists think the Giga was a little bigger than the T. rex and some think the T. rex was smarter than the Giga. So what's better? Size or smarts?

★ The Giganotosaurus lived thirty million years <u>BEFORE</u> the T. rex and on different continents. They could never have actually fought each other... <u>UNTIL TODAY!</u>

MY PLAN:

★ ★ ★ ★ ★ ★ ★ ★ ★ ★ ★

<u>I need to find a way to get the Giganotosaurus and the T. rex to fight... at the MUSEUM!</u>

★ ★ ★ ★ ★ ★ ★ ★ ★ ★ ★

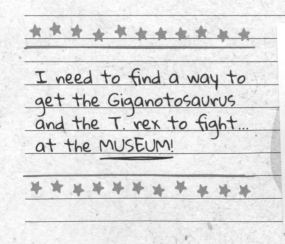

FIELD NOTES:

1. First attempt = <u>FAIL</u>. They got distracted by a herd of Edmontosaurus.

2. Second attempt = <u>FAIL</u>. They both ran after a Futalognkosaurus.

3. I think the Giga and T. rex are both more interested in food than fighting each other, so... I'll make them fight over a bag of beef jerky!

4. Watching these two dino giants fight is <u>AMAZING!</u> The T. rex got the jerky and won the fight!

95

FINDING:

The T. rex beat the Giganotosaurus in the fight, maybe she used her bigger brains to outsmart the Giga!

GIGANTORAPTOR

THEROPOD

(Jie-gant-oh-rap-tor)
Means "Giant Seizer"

96

252 Million	201 Million	145 Million
TRIASSIC	JURASSIC	

Lived in what is now China!

WHEN THEY LIVED

US

| CRETACEOUS | 66 Million PALEOGENE | 23 Million NEOGENE | 2.6 Million QUATERNARY |

GIGANTORAPTOR

Had long sharp claws...
I wonder what for!

Future dino experiment!

★ As long as a truck.

★ Weighed as much as 12 panda bears.

Long legs!

Might have been a fast runner!

to other members of its clade, Gigantoraptor was at least fifty times heavier than other oviraptorosaurs, like Oviraptor.

Related to the famous dinosaur Oviraptor.

Me vs. Gigantoraptor

DINO EXPERIMENT 713

QUESTION: Does the Gigantoraptor have the biggest claws and teeth of all the raptors?

BACKGROUND RESEARCH NOTES:

All raptors have super sharp claws and teeth, so my hypothesis is that since the Gigantoraptor is the biggest, his teeth and claws are the biggest too!

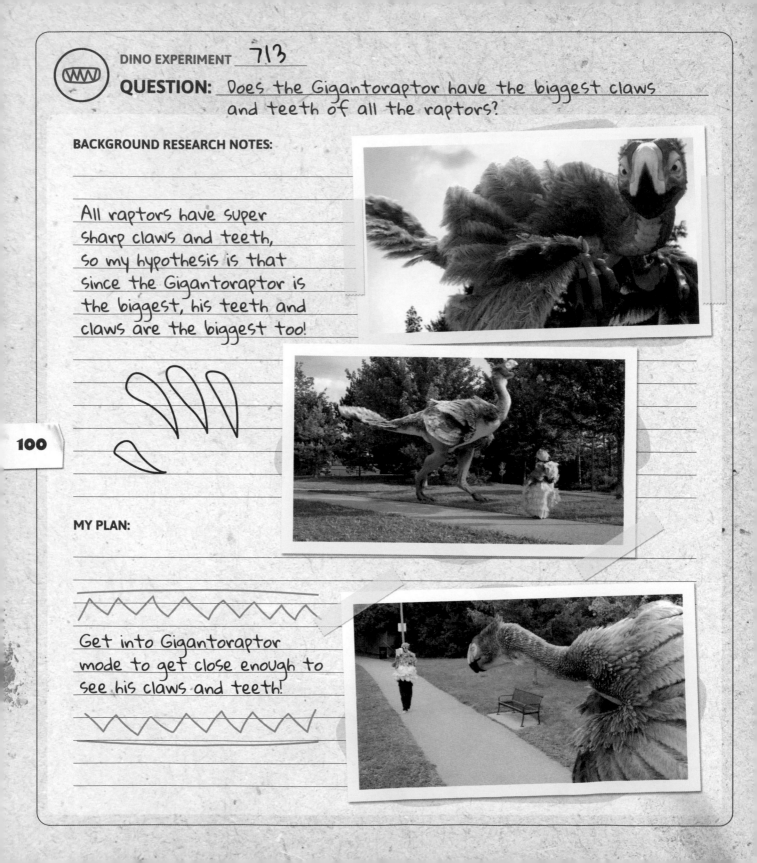

MY PLAN:

Get into Gigantoraptor mode to get close enough to see his claws and teeth!

FIELD NOTES:

1. I got up close and the Gigantoraptor definitely has really long claws, so the first part of my hypothesis was right!

2. The Gigantoraptor squawked at me so I could see his teeth!
   » Update = He squawked but I was <u>TOO SHORT</u> to see his teeth because he was eating leaves from a tree... which is really weird because I thought all raptors were carnivores!

3. Dad put me on his shoulders so I was tall enough to see into the Giga's mouth. I discovered that my hypothesis was wrong! The Gigantoraptor doesn't have <u>ANY</u> teeth in his beak!

4. I thought I had discovered the first toothless, herbivore raptor, but I was wrong again! The Gigantoraptor isn't a raptor. He's an oviraptorosaur which are feathered herbivores that aren't related to raptors at all!!

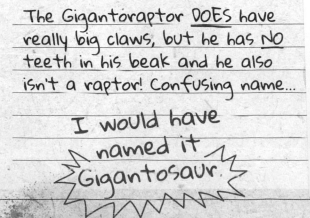101

FINDING:

The Gigantoraptor <u>DOES</u> have really big claws, but he has <u>NO</u> teeth in his beak and he also isn't a raptor! Confusing name...

I would have named it Gigantosaur.

HIPPODRACO

(Hip-oh-drake-oh)
Means "Horse Dragon"

102

WHEN THEY
LIVED

252 Million | 201 Million | 145 Million

TRIASSIC | JURASSIC

Lived in in what is
now Utah, USA

103

Shield-shaped teeth

Name means "horse dragon" because it kind of looks like a horse.

Weighed as much as a horse too.

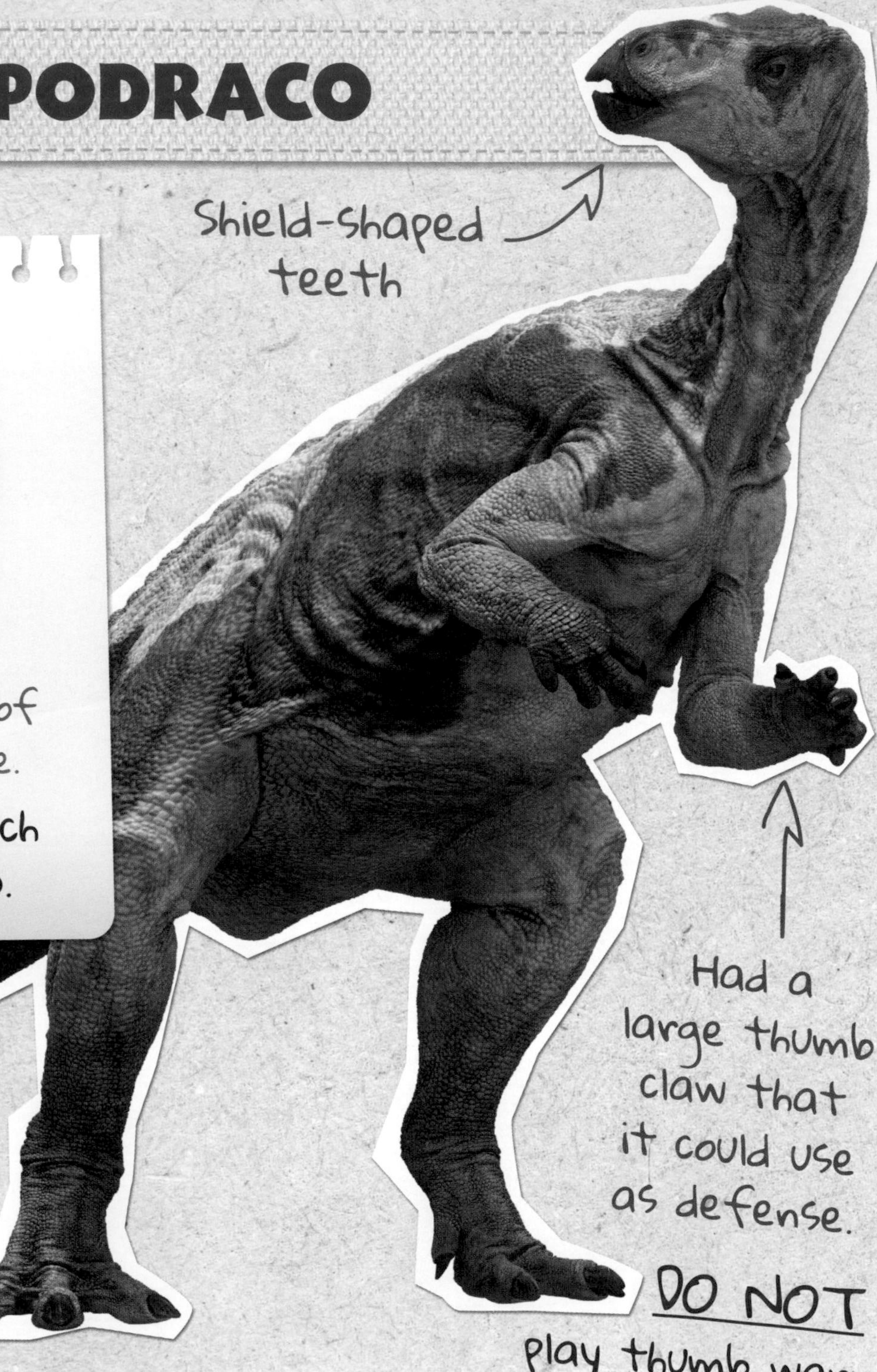

104

Had a large thumb claw that it could use as defense.

DO NOT play thumb war with her!

Only one set of bones has ever been found.

Walked mostly on four legs.

But could run on two.

Me vs. Hippodraco

QUESTION: What does it feel like to ride a Hippodraco?

BACKGROUND RESEARCH NOTES:

★ Hippodraco's name means "Horse Dragon" because his head looks like a horse's head!

★ He also had hoofed toes like a horse, but no mane.

So similar!

MY PLAN:

I need to find a way to get onto the Hippodraco... good thing Saara and I are at Grandma's farm today!

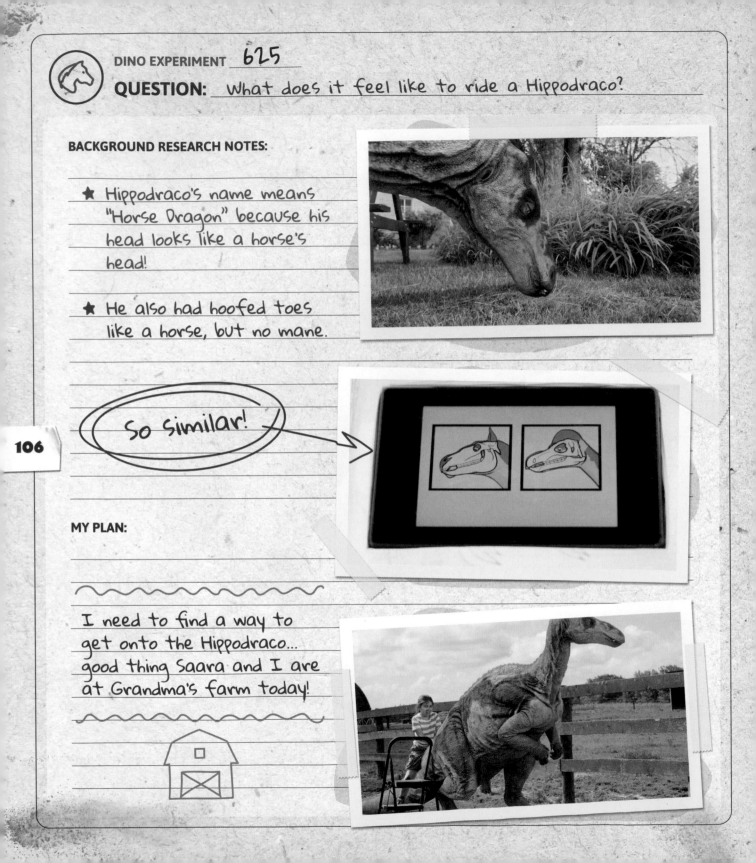

FIELD NOTES:

1. First attempt getting on the Hippodraco = failed. I tried to hop on him from a picnic table but missed. Ouch!

2. Saara asked Grandma to teach us how to ride a horse. You get up using the saddle and then hug the horse with your legs. I wonder if that would work on the Hippodraco?

3. Only one problem... dinosaurs don't have saddles! Grandma says I've got to put both my hands on the Hippodraco's back as I get one leg over! Wish me luck!

>> Update = I got onto a Hippodraco but slid off! Grandma says I need to balance by keeping my back straight, putting weight on my bum, and hugging the Hippodraco with my legs!

4. I did it!!! I got on and stayed on. It was a bumpy but INCREDIBLE ride!

FINDING:

Riding a Hippodraco is a lot like riding a horse... just way harder!

INCISIVOSAURUS

THEROPOD

(In-si-se-vo-sore-us)
Means "Incisor Lizard"

108

WHEN THEY LIVED

252 Million   201 Million   145 Million
TRIASSIC   JURASSIC

Lived in what is now China!

US

┌ 66 Million   ┌ 23 Million   ┌ 2.6 Million
CRETACEOUS   PALEOGENE   NEOGENE   QUATERNARY

INCISIVOSAURUS

Called "incisor lizard" because of its sharp incisors.

Incisor is a sharp tooth used for biting. We have them too!

* As long as two bowling pins.
* Weighed as much as a bowling ball.

INCISIVOSAURUS HAD FRONT TEETH LIKE A BEAVER.

No other dinosaur we know of had teeth like this.

Front teeth good for tearing, other teeth were good for chewing.

Omnivore.

Which means it ate plants AND meat.

Was the size of a turkey.

Me vs. Incisivosaurus

QUESTION: _Did the Incisivosaurus make friends with other Incisivosaurus?_

BACKGROUND RESEARCH NOTES:

Some dinosaurs stick together in groups, I wonder if the Incisivosaurus did that!

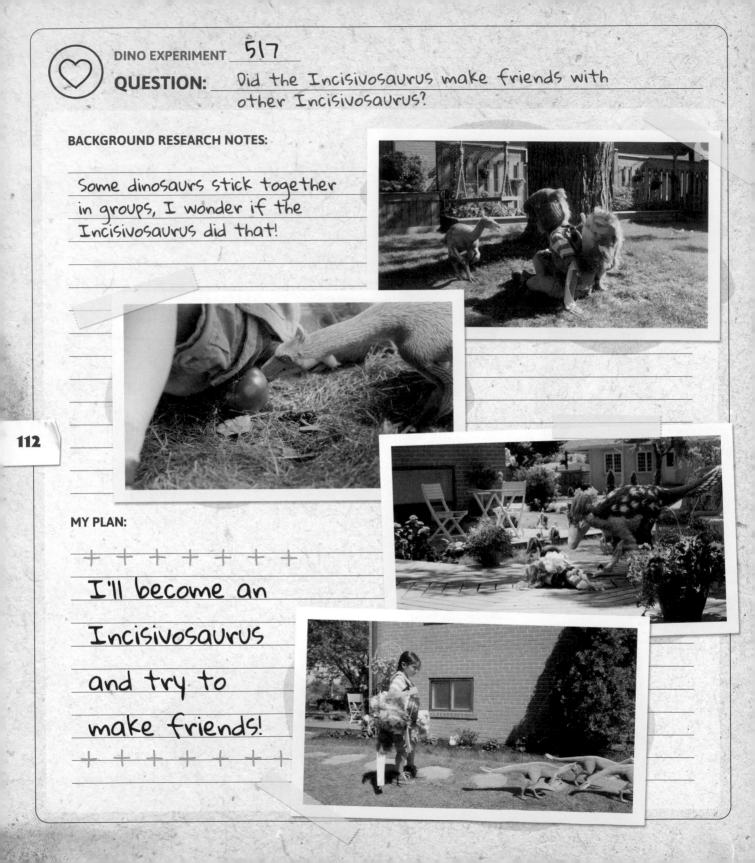

MY PLAN:

+ + + + + + +

I'll become an Incisivosaurus and try to make friends!

+ + + + + + +

FIELD NOTES:

1. I found an Incisivosaurus in my yard. He gave me a tomato and then brought some other Incisivosaurus friends! I'm going to go get some fruits and veggies to share with them!

2. Now we're all working together to watch out for predators. It's easier to keep watch when there's more than one of you. Uh oh! A Dromaeosaurus is here!
   » Update = I threw my Incisivosaurus backpack at the Dromaeosaurus to defend my friends, but without my backpack the Incisivosaurus pack doesn't think I'm one of them.

3. I've put on some Incisivosaurus makeup! Now I'm back in the pack and we all teamed up to scare off the Dromaeosaurus!

Friends again!

FINDING:

The Incisivosaurus make friends so they can find food together, look out for predators, and protect each other.

KENTROSAURUS

ORNITHISCHIA

(Ken-tro-sore-us)
Means "Sharp Point Lizard"

114

WHEN THEY LIVED

252 Million

201 Million

145 Million

TRIASSIC

JURASSIC

66 Million

23 Million

2.6 Million

CRETACEOUS

PALEOGENE

NEOGENE

QUATERNARY

KENTROSAURUS

Kentrosaurus was hard to attack because:

1) Had neck spikes.

2) Had side spikes.

3) Had tail spikes.

Flexible neck, kinda like a turtle!

★ Weighed the same as seven lions!

★ Had more SPIKES than any other Stegosaurid!!

Huge spikes on their shoulders were as long as my leg.

It's tail could swing from side to side

117

Me vs. Kentrosaurus

QUESTION: How did the Kentrosaurus use her bony spikes for defense?

BACKGROUND RESEARCH NOTES:

The Kentrosaurus is
the SPIKIEST of all
the dinosaurs!!

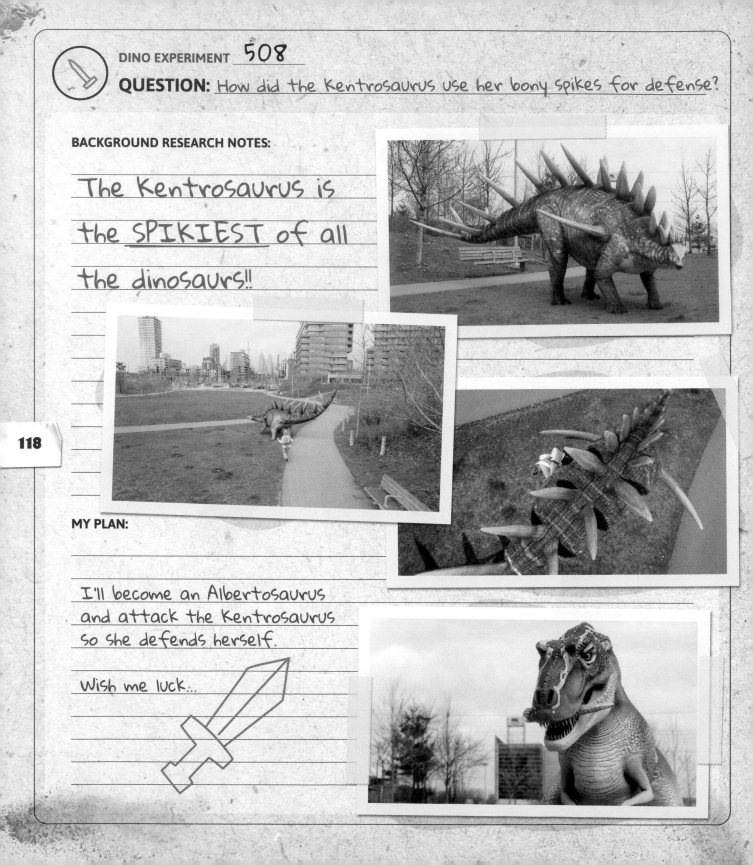

MY PLAN:

I'll become an Albertosaurus
and attack the Kentrosaurus
so she defends herself.

Wish me luck...

FIELD NOTES:

1. As a mighty Albertosaurus, I charged at the Kentrosaurus! The Kentrosaurus defended herself with her spiky tail, her side spikes and then when I threw my backpack she used her back spikes!

2. But while she was distracted with me, a real Albertosaurus snuck up and CHOMPED OFF one of the Kentrosaurus' side spikes!

3. Then, two Dromaeosaurus attacked the Kentrosaurus. So I became a Kentrosaurus to help her scare them off since she lost one of her spikes!

4. I learned dino spikes don't grow back, so I got a cast that the Kentro can use as a spike!

   » When all the predators came back the Kentrosaurus defended herself using her spikes, including the one I got her!

FINDING:

The Kentrosaurus defended itself with spikes on its side, back, AND tail! But they don't grow back!

KOSMOCERATOPS

(Koz-mo-ser-ah-tops)
Means "Decoration Horn Face"

ORNITHISCHIA

Lived in what is now Utah, USA!

252 Million	201 Million	145 Million
TRIASSIC	JURASSIC	

WHEN THEY LIVED

US

CRETACEOUS | 66 Million | PALEOGENE | 23 Million | NEOGENE | 2.6 Million | QUATERNARY

KOSMOCERATOPS

Their horns and frills can tell you how old they are.

Had both horns and hooks. A horn is a straight spike, while a hook is curved and tends to point downwards.

★ As tall as a horse BUT weighed as much as <u>THREE</u> of them!

Had more horns and spikes than any other ceratopsian

Ten spikes on the frill.

One horn above each eye.

One bump on each cheek.

One horn on the nose.

123

actually not strong enough to use in a fight. The spikes on its head were probably good for showing off to other Kosmoceratops.

Bigger and fancier horns helped boy Kosmos find a mate.

Mate means a partner they can have babies with.

Me vs. Kosmo

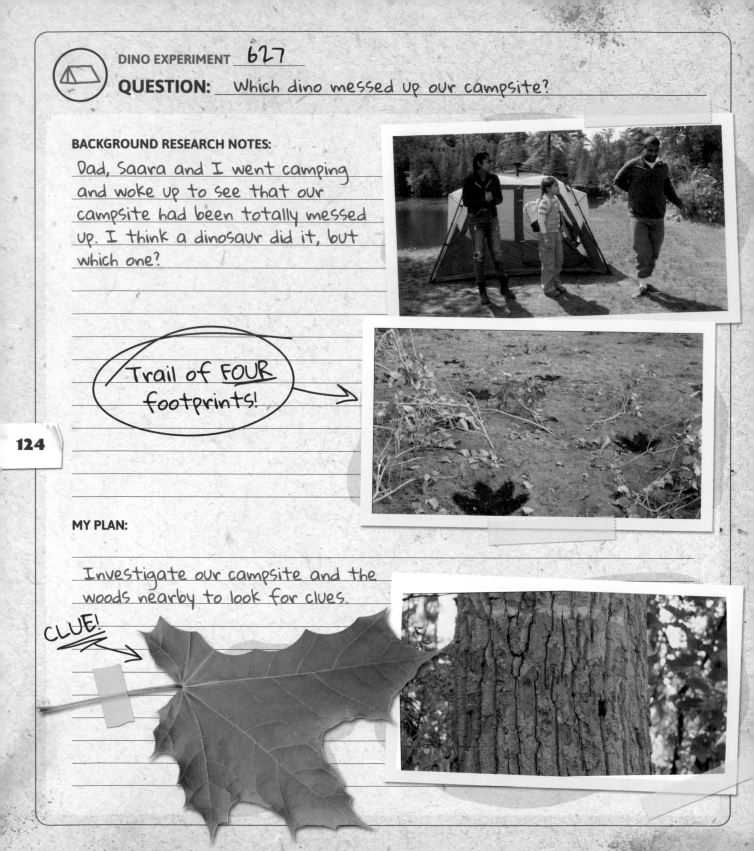

DINO EXPERIMENT __627__

QUESTION: __Which dino messed up our campsite?__

BACKGROUND RESEARCH NOTES:

Dad, Saara and I went camping and woke up to see that our campsite had been totally messed up. I think a dinosaur did it, but which one?

Trail of FOUR footprints!

124

MY PLAN:

Investigate our campsite and the woods nearby to look for clues.

CLUE!

FIELD NOTES:

1. I found clues: a bunch of chewed leaves, bark that was rubbed off a tree, and a trail of four footprints. The dino that did it is a herbivore with lots of horns or spikes that walks on four legs!

2. I followed the footprints and saw the Dracorex! He's a herbivore with spikes, but only walks on two legs, not four. So it wasn't him.

3. Next, I met the Triceratops. She's a herbivore with three horns who walks on four legs. BUT, the tree with bark rubbed off had way more marks than she could make. She didn't make the mess.

4. That's when I found the Kosmoceratops. She's a herbivore who walks on all fours and has more horns than any other ceratopsian! Her horns even match the markings at our campsite. She's the dino that did it!

FINDING:

The Kosmoceratops is the dino that messed up our campsite because she's a herbivore, walks on all fours, and has tons of horns!

MAIASAURA

ORNITHISCHIA

(My-ah-sore-ah)
Means "Good Mother Lizard"

Because they brought food back for their babies.

126

252 Million

201 Million

145 Million

TRIASSIC

JURASSIC

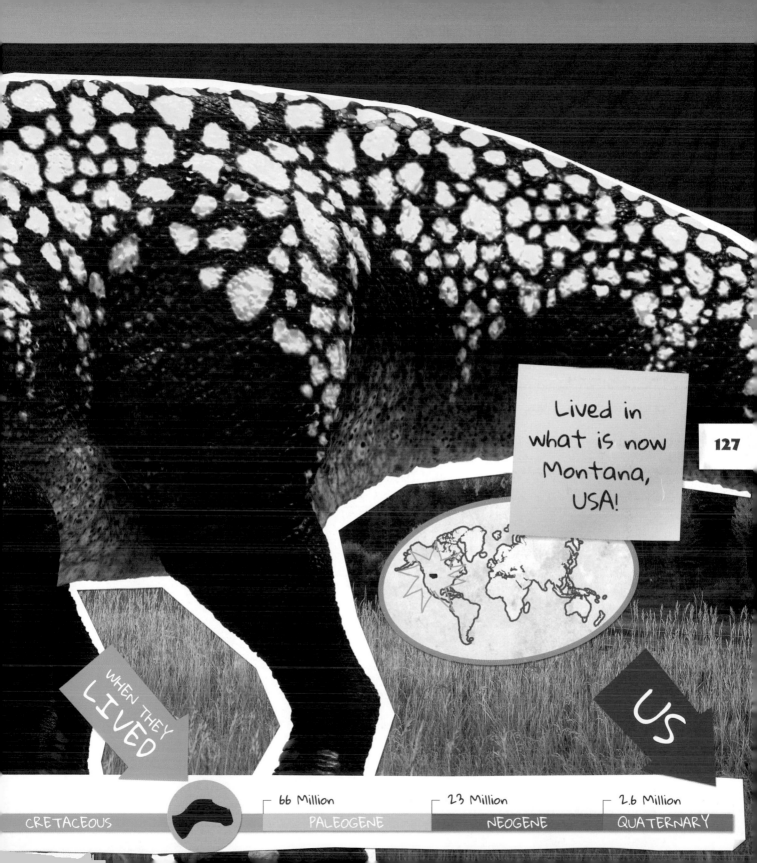

MAIASAURA

From the duck-billed dinosaur family!

>Yum!<

★ Ate leaves and maybe some rotten wood!

★ Height of three deer, length of six deer.

Parents took care of babies until they could take care of themselves, like people do!

> But most babies got eaten before they even turned one year old! Poor baby dinos...

Laid thirty to forty round eggs at a time.

Eggs were about the size of ostrich eggs.

Many bones of adults and juveniles, as well as eggs and nests.

Maiasaura lived in big herds.

As many as 10,000 dinos!

Me vs. Maiasaura

NASA sent their bones into space... just for fun!

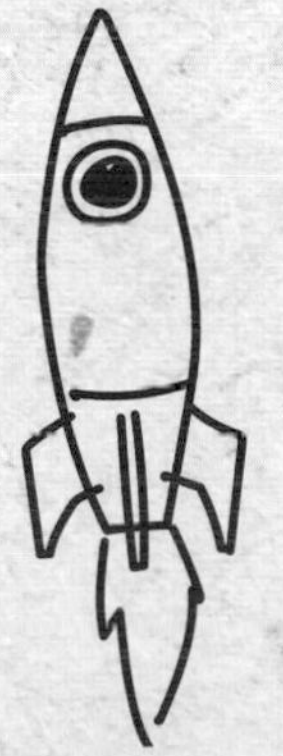

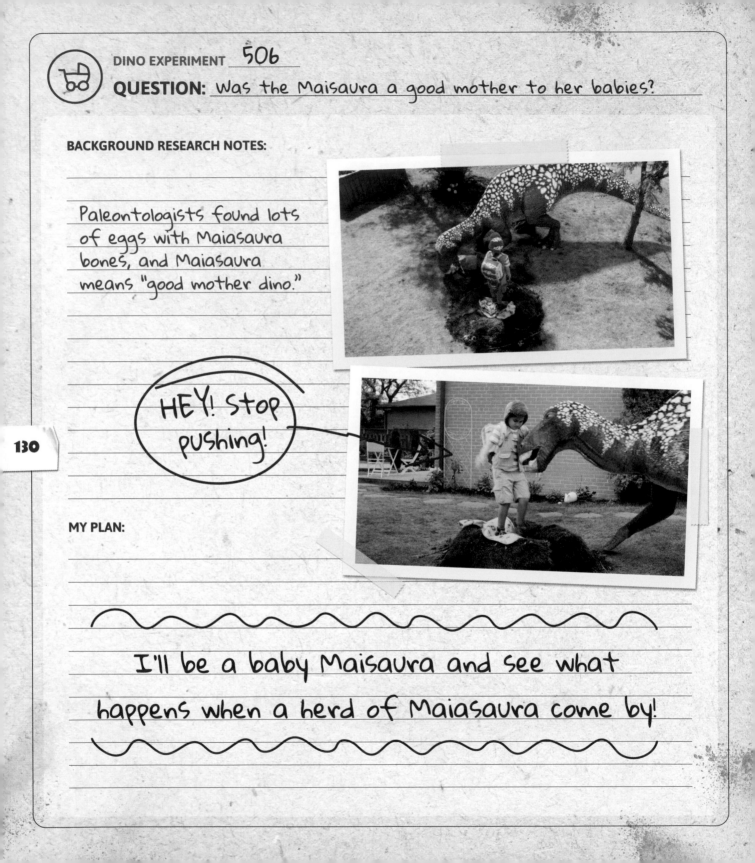

DINO EXPERIMENT 506

QUESTION: Was the Maisaura a good mother to her babies?

BACKGROUND RESEARCH NOTES:

Paleontologists found lots of eggs with Maiasaura bones, and Maiasaura means "good mother dino."

HEY! STOP PUSHING!

MY PLAN:

I'll be a baby Maisaura and see what happens when a herd of Maiasaura come by!

FIELD NOTES:

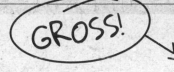

1. A Maiasaura mom noticed me then chewed up lettuce and SPIT IT UP on me! Ewww so much for being a good mother!
   » Update = My mom told me she chewed up food for me when I was a baby to help me eat. The Maiasaura mom was helping me eat!

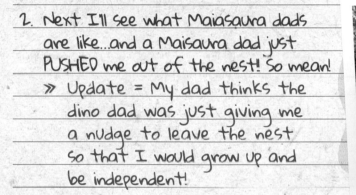

2. Next I'll see what Maiasaura dads are like...and a Maiasaura dad just PUSHED me out of the nest! So mean!
   » Update = My dad thinks the dino dad was just giving me a nudge to leave the nest so that I would grow up and be independent!

3. Now a hungry T. rex is here... I wonder which one will protect me!
   » Update = My Maiasaura parents worked TOGETHER! The mom took on the T. rex while the dad made sure I was safe!

FINDING:

The mom and dad Maiasaura are both great parents! They fed me, taught me to be on my own, and protected me from a T. rex too!

MICRORAPTOR

THEROPOD

(Mie-kro-rap-tor)
Means "Small Thief"

WHEN THEY LIVED

| ⌐252 Million | | ⌐201 Million | | ⌐145 M |
| TRIASSIC | | | JURASSIC | |

Lived in what is now China!

US

| CRETACEOUS | 66 Million | 23 Million | 2.6 Million |
| | PALEOGENE | NEOGENE | QUATERNARY |

MICRORAPTOR

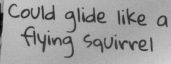
Could glide like a flying squirrel

★ Tiny! As heavy as a can of soup!

★ Paleontologists have found hundreds of fossils of the Microraptor.

The more bones we find, the more we can learn!

Called small thief because they were one of the smallest dinos ever discovered!

Hungry like my little brother!
Fossils have been found with fish, birds, and lizards in their bellies.

① ② ③ ④

135

Had four wings.

Me vs. Micro

Wingspan was as long as my arms stretched out.

Wingspan means the length from the tip of one wing to the other.

QUESTION: How did the Microraptor protect himself from predators?

BACKGROUND RESEARCH NOTES:

The Microraptor is one of the smallest dinosaurs ever discovered.

The microraptor was small but fierce.

MY PLAN:

Observe how a Microraptor protects himself from an Ozraptor!

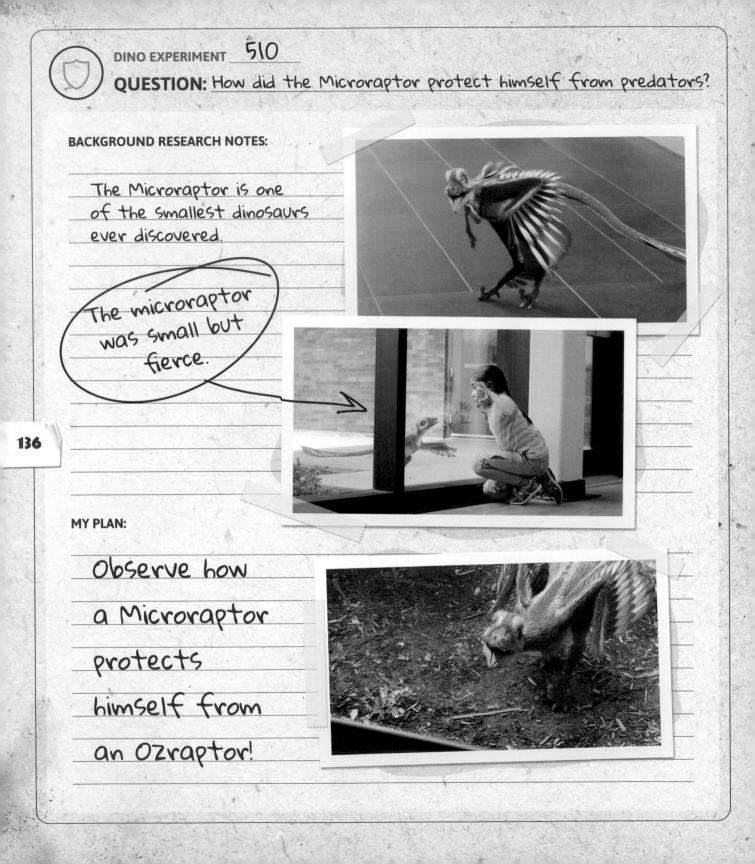

FIELD NOTES:

1. The Ozraptor goes after the distracted Microraptor but the Microraptor uses his speed to dodge around the Ozraptor!

2. But the Microraptor can't run forever... the Ozraptor is gaining on him!
   » Update = The Microraptor used his small size to escape and climb up out of the Ozraptor's reach.

3. Now more Microraptors have come to help scare off the Ozraptor!

FINDING:

The Microraptor uses speed, small size and teamwork to escape from predators! Bigger isn't always better—remember, big dinosaurs went extinct but small dinosaurs survived and evolved into birds.

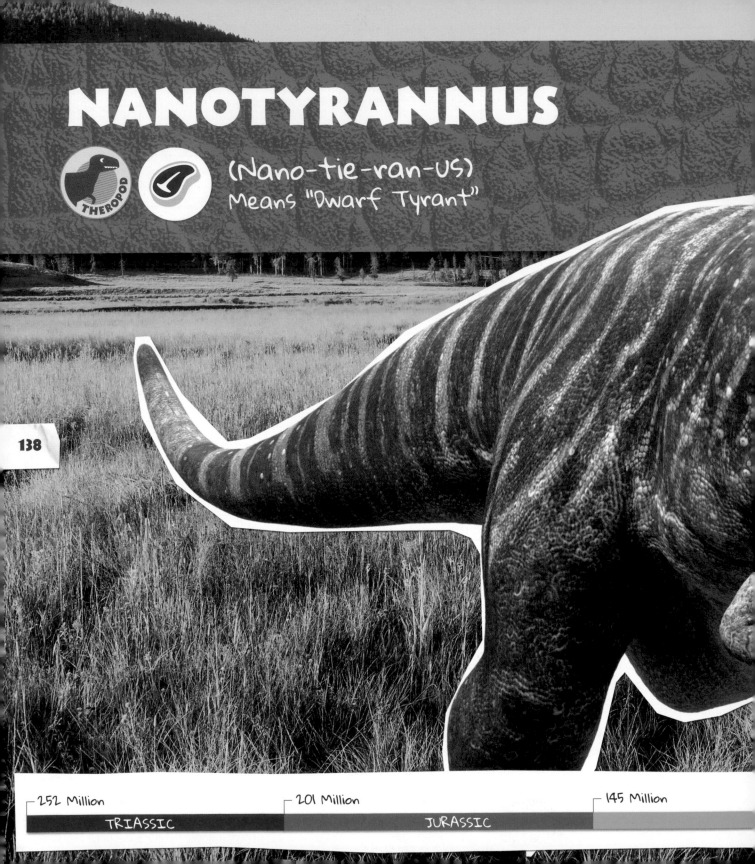

NANOTYRANNUS

THEROPOD

(Nano-tie-ran-us)
Means "Dwarf Tyrant"

252 Million
TRIASSIC

201 Million
JURASSIC

145 Million

139

Lived in what is now the Western United States

WHEN THEY LIVED

US

CRETACEOUS		66 Million		23 Million		2.6 Million
			PALEOGENE		NEOGENE	QUATERNARY

NANOTYRANNUS

Only one small skull has ever been discovered.

★ Length of three bears and as tall as a bear standing. Up.

★ Called a dwarf tyrant because it was one of the smallest tyrannosaurids

This is food Dexter threw. It's <u>NOT</u> related to any Nanotyrannus experiments.

<u>Tyrannosauridae</u>

is the family of dinosaurs that the Nanotyrannus, Albertosaurus, and T. rex belong to.

There is some debate over whether Nanotyrannus is its own dinosaur or just a smaller Tyrannosaurus Rex.

Why?

They look the same BUT T. rex had more growth rings than the Nano.

What are growth rings?

Rings in bones that help paleontologists figure out how old a dinosaur is.

Trees have growth rings too!

Me vs. Nano

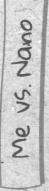

DINO EXPERIMENT **827**

QUESTION: Is the Nanotyrannus actually just a kid T. rex?

BACKGROUND RESEARCH NOTES:

Nanotyrannus

T. rex

=

?

★ Some Paleontologists now believe fossils they thought belonged to different dinosaurs might belong to the same dinosaur, just at different ages!

★ No kid T. rex fossils have been found, so it's possible the Nanotyrannus is a kid T. rex.

MY PLAN:

x x x x x x x x x x x x x x x x x x x x x x

Put a T. rex and Nanotyrannus together and see how they react. If they try to kill each other, they probably aren't related!

x x x x x x x x x x x x x x x x x x

FIELD NOTES:

1. I see the Nanotyrannus approaching the T. rex. He's smaller than the T. rex, which makes sense if the Nano is the kid!

2. The two dinos get close and they don't try to kill each other. What does that mean?

3. A Quetzalcoatlus is here and goes after the T. rex, oh no!
   » Update = The Nano attacked the Quetz and helped save the T. rex!

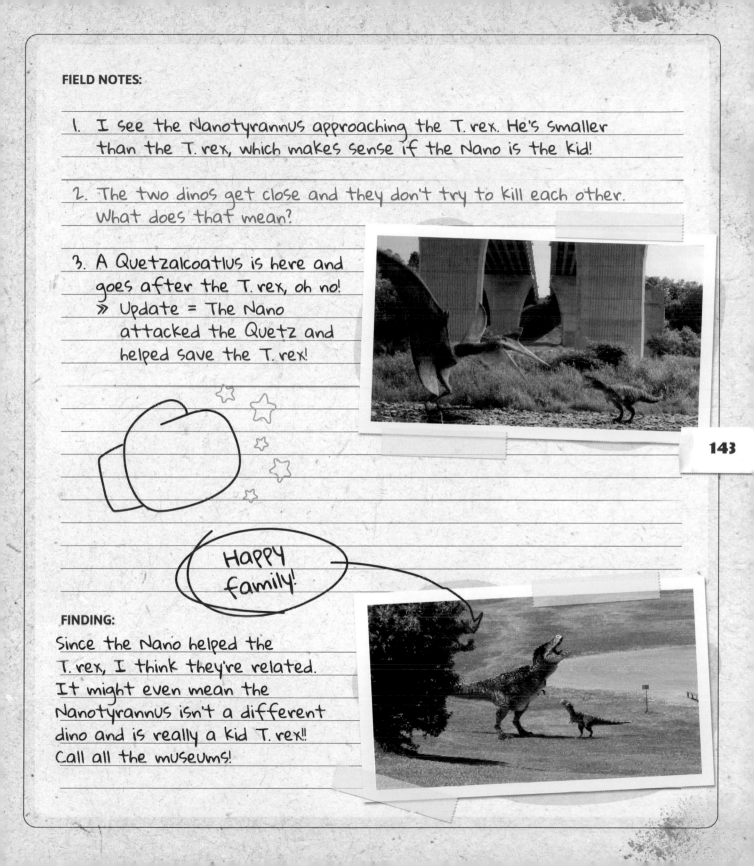

143

Happy family!

FINDING:

Since the Nano helped the T. rex, I think they're related. It might even mean the Nanotyrannus isn't a different dino and is really a kid T. rex!! Call all the museums!

NANUQSAURUS

(Nah-nuk-sore-us)
Means "Polar Bear Lizard"

144

252 Million	201 Million	145 Million
TRIASSIC	JURASSIC	

Lived in what is now Alaska, USA!

145

WHEN THEY LIVED

US

| CRETACEOUS | 66 Million | 23 Million | 2.6 Million |
| | PALEOGENE | NEOGENE | QUATERNARY |

NANUQSAURUS

Could smell really well!!

This helped them hunt!

146

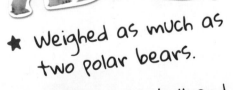

★ Weighed as much as two polar bears.

★ Nanuqsaurus skull and jaw fragments were first found in 2006 at the North Slope of Alaska.

"Nanuq" is the Inupiat word for polar bear. Got that name because it lived in cold places, like polar bears!

Alaska might not have been as cold then as it is now, but it was still cooler than a lot of places dinosaurs lived.

Had good eyesight because it was dark for most of the day.

me vs. Nanuqsaurus.

DINO EXPERIMENT __804__

QUESTION: ___How do dinosaurs keep warm in the winter?___

BACKGROUND RESEARCH NOTES:

Different dinosaurs have
different ways of staying
warm when it's cold outside.

148

MY PLAN:

Go outside and observe
how different dinosaurs
stay warm when it's
really cold out.

FIELD NOTES:

1. I became a Nanuqsaurus and got close enough to discover that the Nanuq has two layers of feathers: a top layer that keeps him dry and a bottom layer that keeps him super warm!

2. Next, I became a Dromaeosaurus and followed the Dromy into our shed where she made a little den out of our old junk. It's pretty toasty in there!

3. Then I became an Incisivosaurus and three Incisivos let me get close and hide together with them to keep warm. It is cozy when you're snuggled up with three little dinos!

149

FINDING:

★ Nanuqsaurus keep warm in the winter because they have layers of feathers just like ducks and geese.

★ Dromaeosaurus keep warm by staying in a den just like bears, foxes, and penguins.

★ Incisivosaurus keep warm by huddling together just like lions and chickadees.

OZRAPTOR

THEROPOD

(OZ-rap-tor)
Means "Australian Thief"

150

WHEN THEY LIVED

|— 252 Million |— 201 Million |— 145 Million
TRIASSIC   JURASSIC

Lived in
what is now
Australia!

US

CRETACEOUS	66 Million	23 Million	2.6 Million
	PALEOGENE	NEOGENE	QUATERNARY

OZRAPTOR

Named "Australian Thief" because it was found in what is now Australia.

The Lizard of Oz!

✱ Very small dino, weighed about as much as a tree-kangaroo.

↖ Have only found one shin bone, but it's different than any other dino shin bone ever discovered.

* Oldest *
known dinosaur
that has
been found in
Australia.

Found by some
school kids!
One day I want to
discover a dinosaur!

**NOT RELATED TO OTHER "RAPTOR"
DINOSAURS LIKE VELOCIRAPTOR.**

"Raptor" just
means robber
and is used for
lots of dinosaur
names.

Me vs. Ozzie

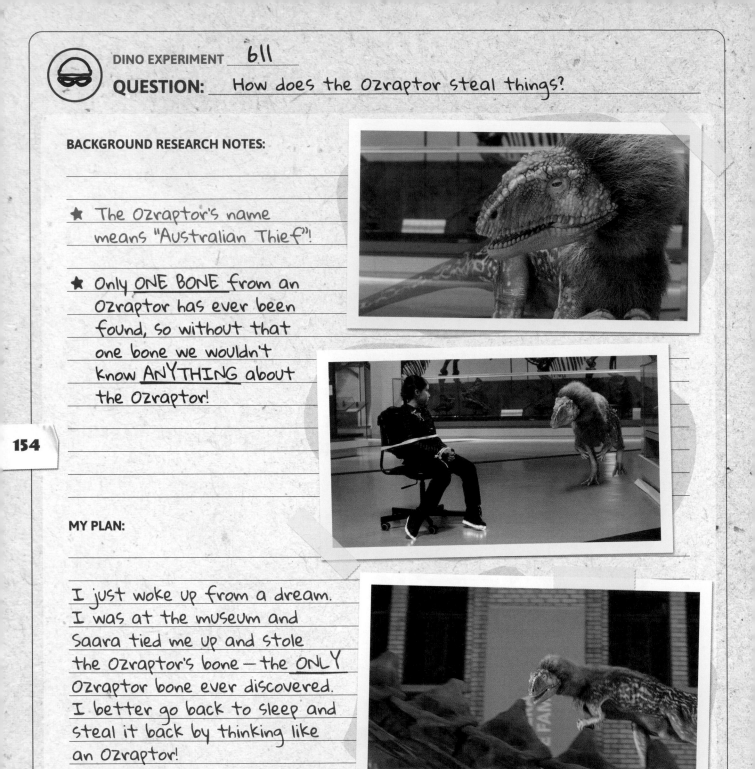

DINO EXPERIMENT ___611___

QUESTION: How does the Ozraptor steal things?

BACKGROUND RESEARCH NOTES:

★ The Ozraptor's name means "Australian Thief"!

★ Only ONE BONE from an Ozraptor has ever been found, so without that one bone we wouldn't know ANYTHING about the Ozraptor!

MY PLAN:

I just woke up from a dream. I was at the museum and Saara tied me up and stole the Ozraptor's bone — the ONLY Ozraptor bone ever discovered. I better go back to sleep and steal it back by thinking like an Ozraptor!

154

FIELD NOTES:

1. Back to sleep...
   » I used my Ozraptor pin to cut through the rope to get out! But Evil Dream Saara still got away...

2. I'm awake!
   » Real Saara just had a great idea to defeat Evil Dream Saara—I need to move as fast as an Ozraptor!

3. Back to sleep...
   » I activate my Ozraptor roller skates to go super fast and catch up to Saara, but she just used rocket shoes to fly away. Nooo!

4. I'm awake!
   » Real Saara helped me figure out that even though the Ozraptor can't fly, he can climb AND jump!

5. Back to sleep...
   » I activated my Ozraptor springs! I jump up to grab the bone back from Evil Dream Saara and then a real Ozraptor climbed up to capture her!

FINDING:

The Ozraptor used his speed as well as climbing and jumping abilities to steal things!

PACHYCEPHALOSAURUS

ORNITHISCHIA

(Pah-key-sef-ah-lo-sore-us)
Means "Thick-headed Lizard"

156

252 Million	201 Million	145 Million
TRIASSIC	JURASSIC	

Lived all over what is now the Western USA and Alberta, Canada

WHEN THEY LIVED

US

| CRETACEOUS | 66 Million PALEOGENE | 23 Million NEOGENE | 2.6 Million QUATERNARY |

PACHYCEPHALOSAURUS

Their dome (which was tall, visible, and maybe colored) may have had a similar purpose as a male peacock's tail—to impress females or to intimidate rival males.

The dome was as tall as a soccer ball!!!

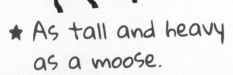

★ As tall and heavy as a moose.

★ Had fancy-looking bumps at the back of its skull dome.

Lived with T. rex and Triceratops.

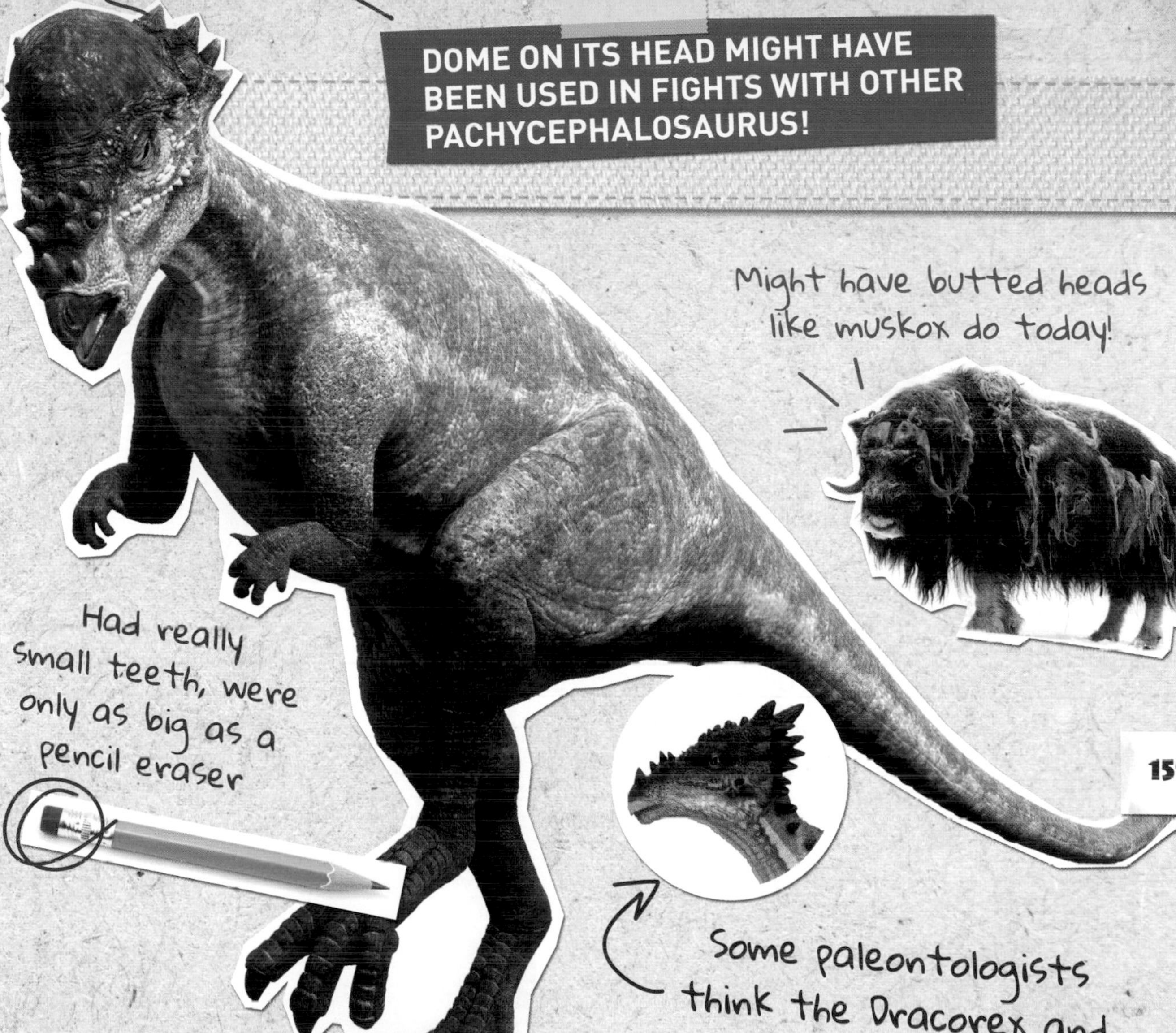

DOME ON ITS HEAD MIGHT HAVE BEEN USED IN FIGHTS WITH OTHER PACHYCEPHALOSAURUS!

Might have butted heads like muskox do today!

Had really small teeth, were only as big as a pencil eraser

Some paleontologists think the Dracorex and Stygimoloch are kid and Teen versions of the Pachycephalosaurus!

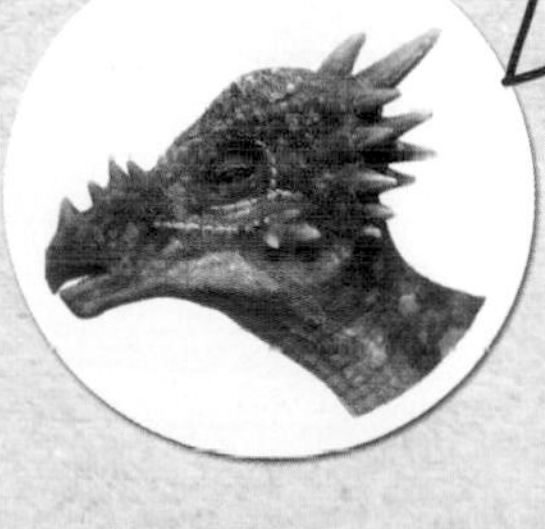

Me vs. Pachycephalosaurus

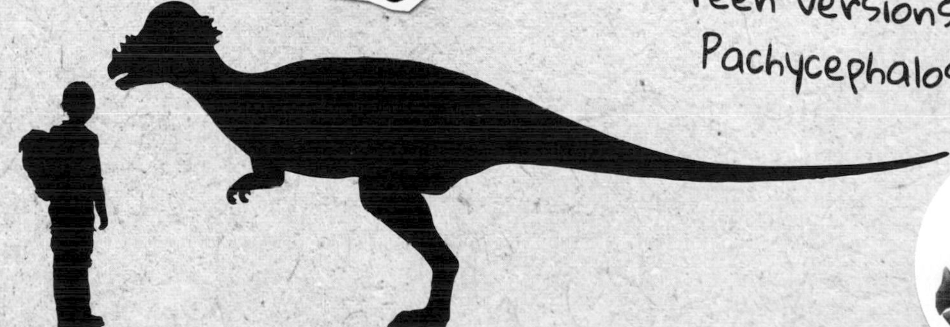

DINO EXPERIMENT _828_

QUESTION: Are the Dracorex and Stygimoloch actually just younger Pachycephalosaurus?

BACKGROUND RESEARCH NOTES:

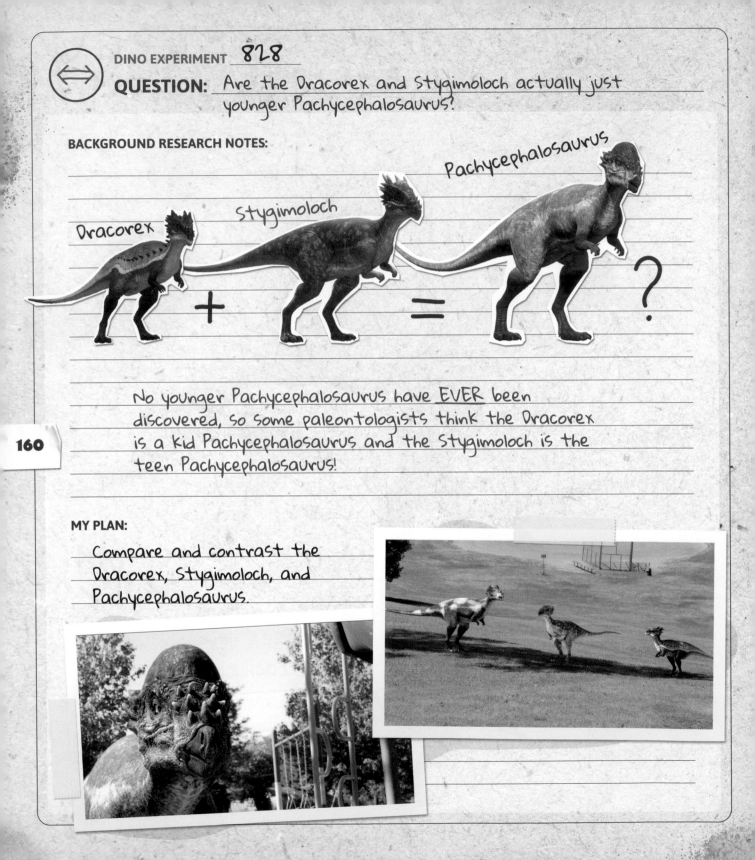

Dracorex

Stygimoloch

Pachycephalosaurus

+ = ?

No younger Pachycephalosaurus have _EVER_ been discovered, so some paleontologists think the Dracorex is a kid Pachycephalosaurus and the Stygimoloch is the teen Pachycephalosaurus!

160

MY PLAN:

Compare and contrast the Dracorex, Stygimoloch, and Pachycephalosaurus.

FIELD NOTES:

1. Similarities:
   » Lived during the Cretaceous period.
   » Lived in North America.
   » Were herbivores.
   » Had bumps on their noses.
   » Had short arms and walked on two legs.

2. Differences:
   » Their heads and their spike sizes.
   » The Dracorex is the smallest and has no dome and medium spikes.
   » The Stygimoloch is mid-size and has a small dome and big spikes.
   » The Pachycephalosaurus is the biggest and has a big dome and small spikes.

3. I didn't know how to solve this one, so I went to the museum and saw cassowary bird skulls.

   » The cassowary skulls are different sizes and look different, BUT they're all from the same bird, just at different ages.
   » So even though the Dracorex, Stygimoloch, and Pachycephalosaurus skulls are different it might be because the Dracorex and Stygimoloch are still growing!

FINDING:

Even though there are differences between these dinos, there are more ways that they are alike! Therefore I think the Dracorex and Stygimoloch are younger Pachycephalosaurus! See! New discoveries happen ALL THE TIME!

cassowary bird skulls

PSITTACOSAURUS

162

ORNITHISCHIA

(Sit-ah-ko-sore-us)
Means "Parrot Lizard"

WHEN THEY LIVED

252 Million
TRIASSIC

201 Million
JURASSIC

145 Mi

PSITTACOSAURUS

Called a parrot lizard because its beak looks like a parrot's

Quills were as long as a ruler.

Was named by the same person who named the T. rex and Velociraptor, Henry Fairfield Osborn.

★ Weighed as much as an orangutan.

★ As tall as a Komodo dragon.

One of the earliest members of the horned dinosaur family.

But no horns on the nose or above the eyes...

Babies hung out in groups.

Maybe even in underground homes!

Swallowed stones to help them digest their food.

Had scales on most of the body, but long quills like bristles on the top of the tail.

Me vs. Psittacosaurus

Like a squirrel's bushy tail!

QUESTION: ___How does the Psittacosaurus defend himself?___

BACKGROUND RESEARCH NOTES:

The Psittacosaurus has quills on his tail, but I'm not sure if or how they used them!

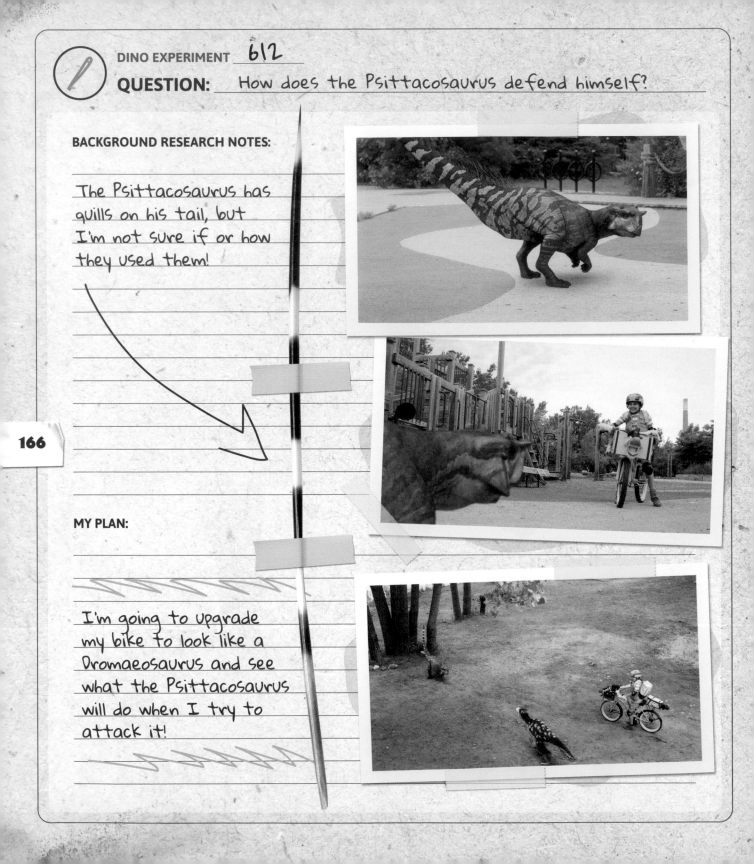

MY PLAN:

I'm going to upgrade my bike to look like a Dromaeosaurus and see what the Psittacosaurus will do when I try to attack it!

FIELD NOTES:

1. <u>ATTEMPT ONE:</u> I tried riding after the Psittacosaurus but he didn't do anything. My bike needs a Dromaeosaurus upgrade.

2. <u>ATTEMPT TWO:</u> I added a cardboard Dromy face to my bike. He was working—the Psittacosaurus raised his tail, <u>BUT</u> before he could attack the Dromy face fell off.

3. <u>ATTEMPT THREE:</u> This time my bike looked like a Dromy all over but the Psittacosaurus still didn't attack!! <u>WHY?</u>
   » Update = I remembered some predators hunt in packs

4. <u>ATTEMPT FOUR:</u> I called another Dromy and the Psittacosaurus used his tail quills to defend himself!!
   » Update = One of the Psittacosaurus quills popped my tire... <u>WORTH IT!</u>

FINDING:

The Psittacosaurus may have used its tail quills for defense but only if he really feels threatened!

UP<u>DA</u>TE! Paleontologists now think that the quills were more like soft bristles—like a squirrel's tail! These bristles would have made the Psittaco look bigger but would not have helped in a fight.

SINORNITHOSAURUS

THEROPOD

(Sine-or-nith-oh-sore-us)
Means "Chinese Bird Lizard"

252 Million		201 Million		145 Million	
TRIASSIC		JURASSIC			

Lived in what is now China

US

	66 Million		23 Million		2.6 Million
CRETACEOUS		PALEOGENE		NEOGENE	QUATERNARY

SINORNITHOSAURUS

Sinornithosaurus had wings and feathers but likely could not fly.

Maybe it could glide?

Future Dino Experiment!

Great eyesight, could hunt well at night and in the day.

★ As long as a Crane.

Has different types
of feathers!

← Short feathers on head.

One of the first
dinosaurs found
with feathers.

This shows how
birds are related
to dinosaurs!

Medium
feathers →
on body.

↑
Long feathers
on arms.

Me vs. Sino

Hunted small
mammals, reptiles,
and birds.

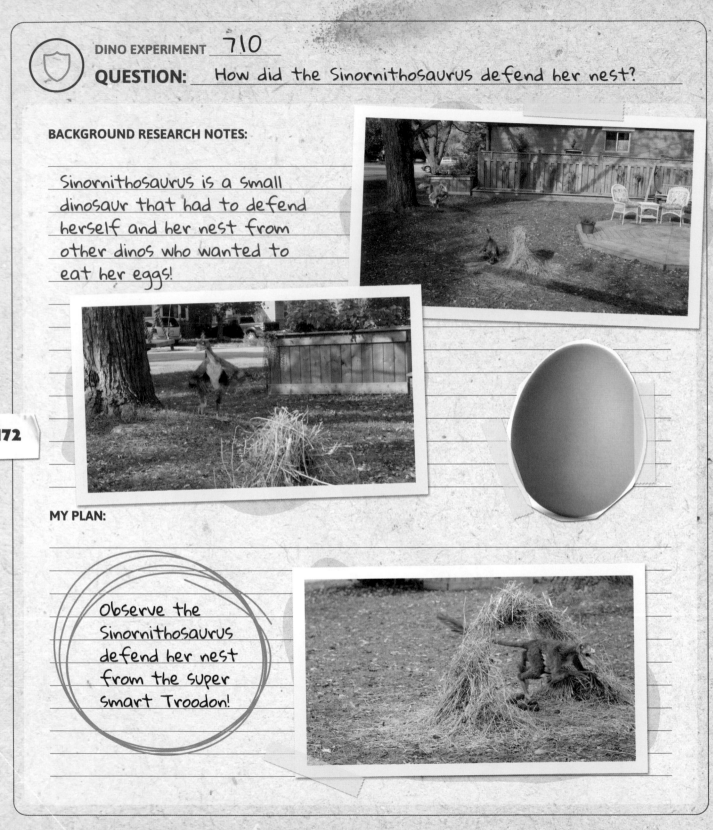

QUESTION: ___How did the Sinornithosaurus defend her nest?___

BACKGROUND RESEARCH NOTES:

Sinornithosaurus is a small dinosaur that had to defend herself and her nest from other dinos who wanted to eat her eggs!

172

MY PLAN:

Observe the Sinornithosaurus defend her nest from the super smart Troodon!

FIELD NOTES:

1. A Troodon is trying to get the eggs from a Sinornithosaurus nest! The Sino goes low and started squawking super <u>LOUD</u> to defend her nest... It worked!
<u>THE TROODON RAN AWAY!</u>

2. The Troodon is back! Now the Sino is leaving her smell all around the nest, when the Troodon smelled the scent he ran away! SO <u>INTERESTING!!</u> Mom says the Sino might be marking her territory like dogs do!

3. Now the Troodon is coming from a different direction where there <u>ISN'T</u> a smell! The Sino is squawking but the Troodon keeps going! This is going to be good!

173

4. The Sinornithosaurus <u>CHARGED</u> at the Troodon, flapping her wings like crazy! The Troodon

FINDING:

<u>The Sinornithosaurus defended her nest by:</u>

★ Squawking loudly.
★ Marking her territory with a scent.
★ Flapping her wings as she charged at predators.

SPINOSAURUS

THEROPOD

(Spy-no-sore-us)
Means "Spine Lizard"

174

Found in what is now Northern Africa

175

WHEN THEY LIVED

US

		66 Million		23 Million		2.6 Million
...EOUS		PALEOGENE		NEOGENE		QUATERNARY

SPINOSAURUS

Spinosaurus spent more time in the water than any other big predatory dinosaurs and was more likely a fish-eater than a land-animal predator.

A little bigger than the T. rex.

Teeth were shaped like cones for fish eating, instead of sharp steak knife teeth in other theropods.

The best Spinosaurus skeleton was destroyed during a war making it hard for paleontologists to study this dinosaur.

Long narrow
snout like a
crocodile!

Long spines on backbone give it its
name—probably were enclosed by skin
to form a sail.

BUT
paleontologists
don't know what
Spinosaurus used
the sail for!

Me vs. Spinosaurus

Future Dino Experiment:
What did Spinos use their sails for?

DINO EXPERIMENT __512__

QUESTION: Can Spinosaurus babies hear from inside their eggs?

BACKGROUND RESEARCH NOTES:

Some dinosaurs don't take
care of their babies after
they hatch, but some might
have taken care of their
babies like birds do.

MY PLAN:

Observe a
Spinosaurus
mama and her
nest of eggs!

FIELD NOTES:

1. The Spinosaurus mama sings to her <u>EGGS!</u> Can the babies in the eggs hear her? Human babies can hear their families, maybe dino babies can too!

2. I croak to the eggs and the babies <u>INSIDE</u> start to shake and croak back! I think they heard me!

3. The babies hatched! I became a Spinosaurus baby and now the mama Spinosaurus is singing to all of us! When the babies sing the song back to her, the mama feeds them!

4. Uh oh! The mama Spino left and a Troodon is coming after the babies!

Birds like chickens also sing a song to their babies in their eggs!

5. I sang the Spinosaurus song and the babies followed me away from the Troodon!! Phew!

FINDING:

<u>Baby Spinosaurus can hear their mom from inside their eggs and they remember what they heard after they hatch!</u>

STEGOSAURUS

ORNITHISCHIA

(Steg-Uh-Sore-US)
Means "Roofed Lizard"

180

Lived all over what is now the Western United States

WHEN THEY **LIVED**

252 Million
TRIASSIC

201 Million
JURASSIC

145 Million

US

CRETACEOUS   66 Million   PALEOGENE   23 Million   NEOGENE   2.6   QUATERNARY

STEGOSAURUS

Plates were huge and diamond-shaped, the biggest of any stegosaurid species.

Plates were good for showing off to other Stegosaurus.

★ Weighed as much as five bison.

Four big spikes at the tip of the tail.

Could swing tail spikes hard enough to puncture the bones of an enemy.

Paleontologists think that an injury in an Allosaurus skeleton might be from a Stegosaurus tail spike!

Me vs. Stegosaurus

Paleontologists once thought that the Stego's brain was only the size of a walnut... but it was really the size of TWO walnuts :)

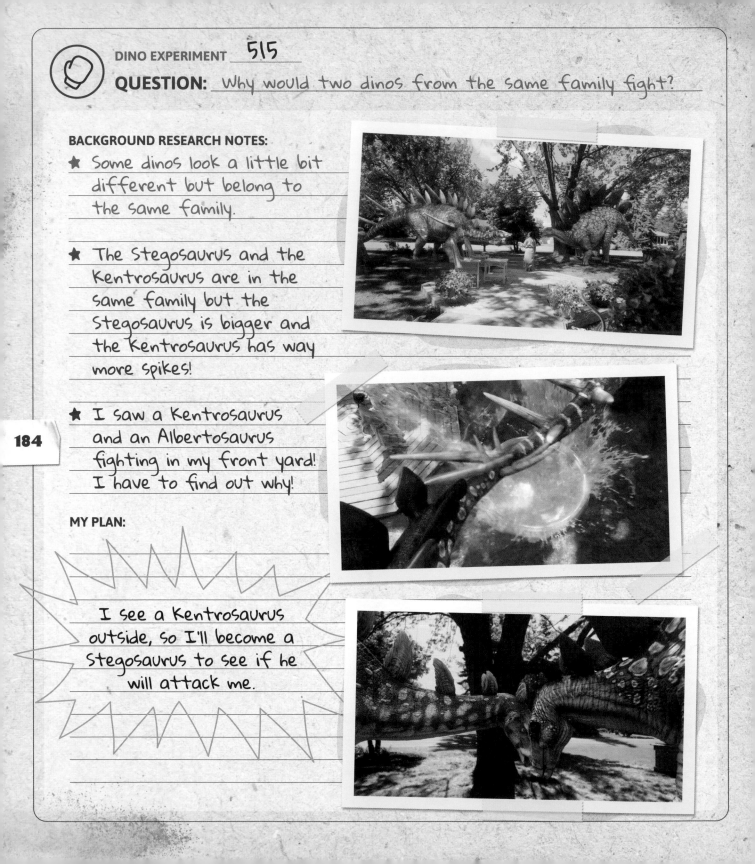

DINO EXPERIMENT **515**

QUESTION: Why would two dinos from the same family fight?

BACKGROUND RESEARCH NOTES:

★ Some dinos look a little bit different but belong to the same family.

★ The Stegosaurus and the Kentrosaurus are in the same family but the Stegosaurus is bigger and the Kentrosaurus has way more spikes!

★ I saw a Kentrosaurus and an Albertosaurus fighting in my front yard! I have to find out why!

MY PLAN:

I see a Kentrosaurus outside, so I'll become a Stegosaurus to see if he will attack me.

FIELD NOTES:

1. The Kentrosaurus was drinking water from Saara's kiddie pool and when I got close he attacked me and destroyed my Stegosaurus costume! But why...

2. Wait! The real Stegosaurus is back and the Stego and Kentro are fighting again!
   » Update = I figured out they're fighting over the water! Not to hurt each other! Just like me and Saara fight over things we don't want to share!

3. I sprayed them with our garden hose so that they can both have a drink. No more fighting!

FINDING:

Some dinosaurs compete for food and water, even ones from the same family! Just like brothers and sisters sometimes fight over stuff.

STYGIMOLOCH

ORNITHISCHIA

(Stij-eh-moll-uk)
Means "Demon from the River Styx"

186

Lived in
what is now the
Western United
States

WHEN THEY
LIVED

US

66 Million	23 Million	2.6 Million
CRETACEOUS	PALEOGENE	NEOGENE	QUATERNARY

STYGIMOLOCH

Just like how the Dracorex might be a kid Pachycephalosaurus!

argument over the lineage of this dinosaur with the latest theory being that the Stygimoloch isn't actually a different dinosaur but is a teenage Pachycephalosaurus that doesn't have a huge dome head yet.

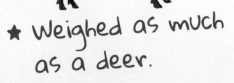

★ Weighed as much as a deer.

★ Might have used their head spikes in fights with other Stygimoloch.

Lived at the same time as the T. rex and Triceratops.

Skull spikes could get as long as a dinner knife!

Two big spikes and many small ones at the back of the head.

Little bumps on the snout.

Smaller, skinnier dome than the Pachycephalosaurus.

Me vs. Stygimoloch

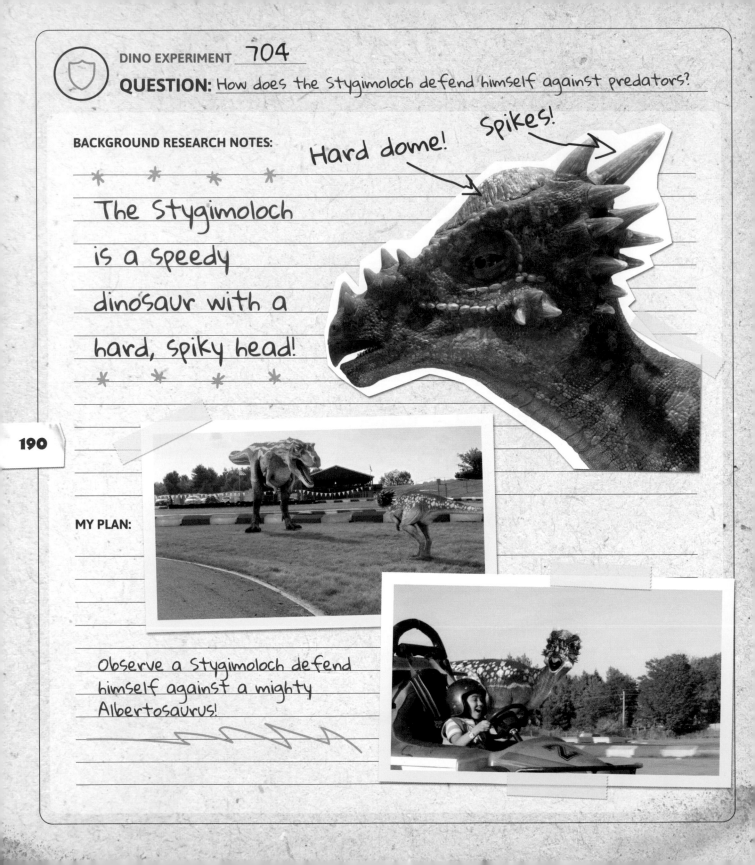

DINO EXPERIMENT __704__

QUESTION: How does the Stygimoloch defend himself against predators?

BACKGROUND RESEARCH NOTES:

Hard dome!

Spikes!

The Stygimoloch is a speedy dinosaur with a hard, spiky head!

190

MY PLAN:

Observe a Stygimoloch defend himself against a mighty Albertosaurus!

FIELD NOTES:

1. The Stygimoloch is being chased by an Albertosaurus! What will happen?
   » Update = The Stygimoloch used a burst of SPEED to get away from the Albertosaurus!

2. Now there are TWO Albertosaurus! Speeding away isn't working...
   » Update = The Stygimoloch DODGES left and right to confuse and avoid the Albertosaurus!

3. Uh oh, now there are THREE Albertosaurus! Dodging isn't working with this many!
   » Update = The Stygimoloch charged and headbutted with his spikes! The Stygimoloch got past three Albertosaurus and ran away!!!

FINDING:

The Stygimoloch defended itself by:

★ Using quick bursts of speed
★ Dodging side to side
★ Headbutting with his spikes

THERIZINOSAURUS

(Thair-uh-zeen-uh-sore-us)
Means "Scythe Lizard"

THEROPOD

192

252 Million	201 Million	145 Million
TRIASSIC	JURASSIC	

Lived in what is now Mongolia!

193

WHEN THEY LIVED

US

| | 66 Million | | 23 Million | | 2.6 Million |
| CRETACEOUS | | PALEOGENE | | NEOGENE | | QUATERNARY |

THERIZINOSAURUS

Longest claws of any animal ever!

Claws were as long as our dog Nixon.

Animal with longest claws alive today is the Giant Armadillo but its claws are only as long as Nixon's nose.

★ Weighed the same as a big elephant.

Laid its eggs with others nearby for safety.

Had feathers, but it couldn't fly...

Me vs. Therizinosaurus

Other possible reasons for feathers:

1) To stay warm.
2) So other dinosaurs would know what kind of dino it was.
3) To tell males from females.

DINO EXPERIMENT ___823___

QUESTION: What do Therizinosaurus do to prove they're the right mate?

BACKGROUND RESEARCH NOTES:

★ Female dinos are often larger than male dinos!

★ Finding a strong mate is important for dinosaurs so that they can have a healthy family.

★ Some male dinosaurs will do a lot to prove they're a good mate

MY PLAN:

♥ ♥ ♥ ♥ ♥ ♥ ♥ ♥

Observe a male and female Therizinosaurus and see if they become partners.

♥ ♥ ♥ ♥ ♥ ♥ ♥ ♥

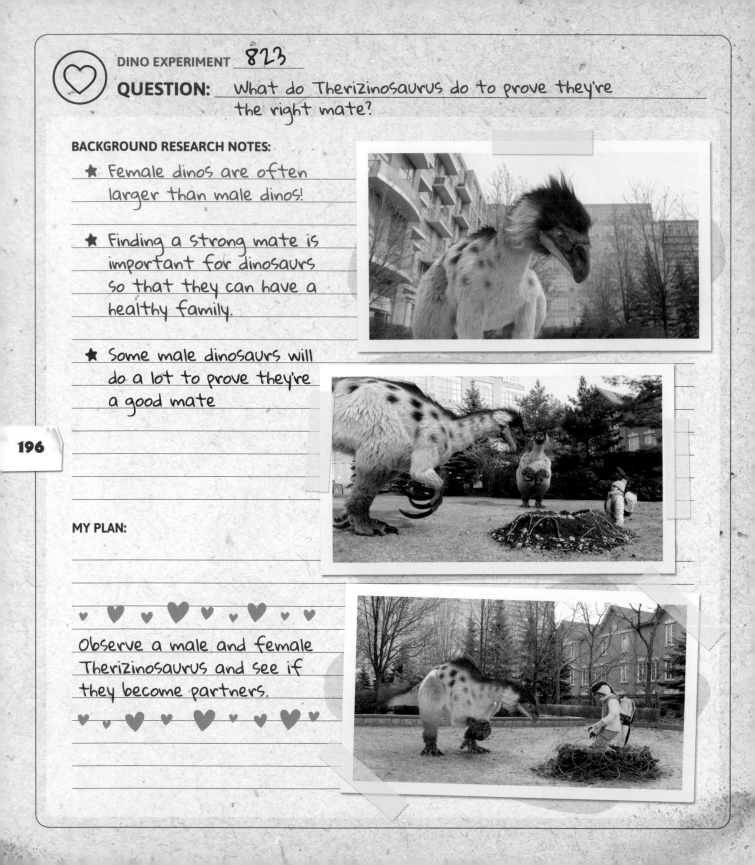

FIELD NOTES:

1. The male Therizinosaurus made a nest for the female but she left him! I guess she didn't like it.

2. I became a Therizino to test it out! Ouch! The nest has too many rocks! I try another one that has too many sticks. I test a third nest made of leaves! It's just right. The real Therizinosaurus female comes back and she likes it so much she stays!

3. Now he's cleaning the female's feathers with his beak! Now she is doing it back to him! Awwww.

4. Next, the male brings the female food then chews it up and spits it into her mouth! Must be dino love!

FINDING:

Therizinosaurus impress each other by:

★ Building nests
★ Cleaning feathers
★ Bringing food

TRICERATOPS

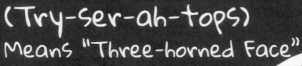

(Try-ser-ah-tops)
Means "Three-horned Face"

252 Million	201 Million	145 Million
TRIASSIC	JURASSIC	

TRICERATOPS

The head frill was probably just used for showing off to other Triceratops.

Dinosaurs love to show off how big and strong they are.

200

* As long as a flatbed truck

* Weighed as much as ten moose.

Had up to eight hundred teeth!
I only have twenty.

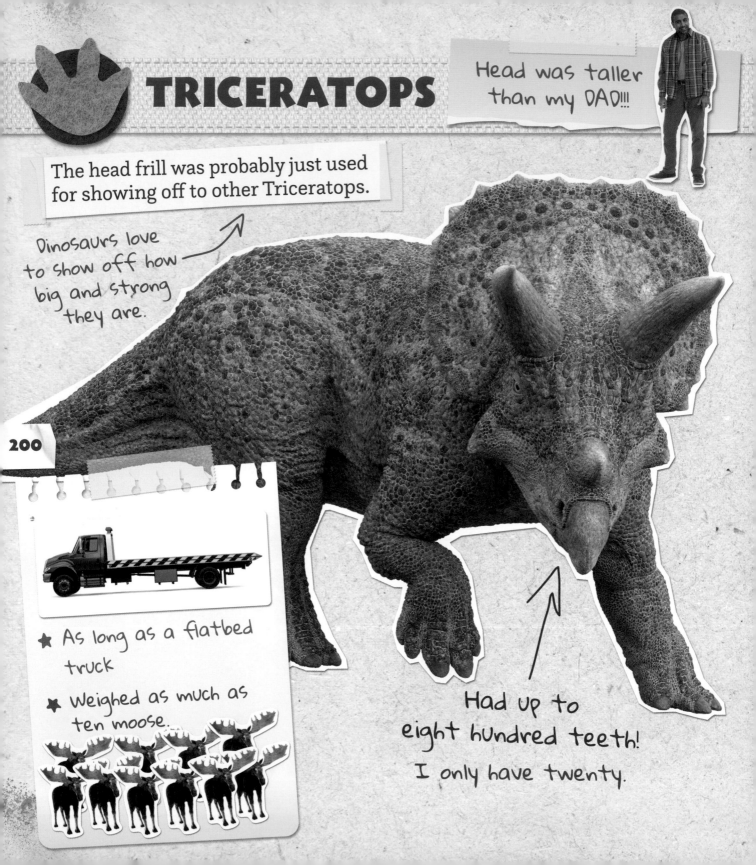

Horns might have been for fighting other Triceratops.

Two horns over the eyes and one small horn on the nose.

Babies had smaller frills and horns that looked different from the adults.

Me vs. Triceratops

Baby Triceratops were only as big as a dog. Sooo cute!

QUESTION: <u>How does the mama Triceratops protect her babies?</u>

BACKGROUND RESEARCH NOTES:

★ Baby Triceratops are easy prey if they're not protected by their mom!

★ Baby Triceratops hatch out of eggs that are as big as a cantaloupe.

Baby Triceratops

MY PLAN:

Become a baby Triceratops and follow a mama Triceratops and her babies!

FIELD NOTES:

1. An Ozraptor attacked, but the mama Triceratops made us huddle under her as she scared off the Ozraptor.

2. Next an Albertosaurus appeared, and the mama Triceratops made us run to safety in different directions while she rammed the Albertosaurus!

3. But then the mama left her nest because it was no longer safe and one baby was left behind! ← Some birds do this too!

   » Update = When we couldn't find the mama Triceratops, the baby was adopted by two mammoths!

Sometimes animals will look after babies from other species! ↗

FINDING:

To keep her babies safe, a mama Triceratops:

★ Huddles over her babies.
★ Takes on a predator while her babies run to safety.
★ Moves her nest if a predator finds it.

TROODON

(Troh-oh-don)
Means "Wounding Tooth"

204

┌ 252 Million   ┌ 201 Million   ┌ 145 Million
TRIASSIC   JURASSIC

Lived in what is now Montana, USA

205

WHEN THEY LIVED

US

CRETACEOUS | 66 Million PALEOGENE | 23 Million NEOGENE | 2.6 Million QUATERNARY

TROODON

It was named "Wounding Tooth" because its teeth had sharp, serrated edges like a saw.
~~Paleontologists now think its teeth look more~~

The first Troodon fossil found was just one tooth!

* Eggs were narrow and long.

* Laid eggs in a dirt nest.

* May have sat on its eggs to protect them.

Baby Troodon left the nest soon after hatching, like ducks and chickens.

Had larger eyes than most dinosaurs which means it might have hunted at night

The eyes of the Troodon were on the front of its face, which means it had <u>BINOCULAR VISION</u> like humans.

Most dinosaurs (especially herbivores) had monocular vision just like modern day prey animals like cows and deer so that they can see what might be trying to hunt them while eating.

Binocular vision is when both your eyes work together to make one image.

As tall as me!

Me vs. vv

Largest brain compared to its size of any dinosaur, about as smart as an ostrich.

QUESTION: How did the Troodon protect her eggs?

BACKGROUND RESEARCH NOTES:

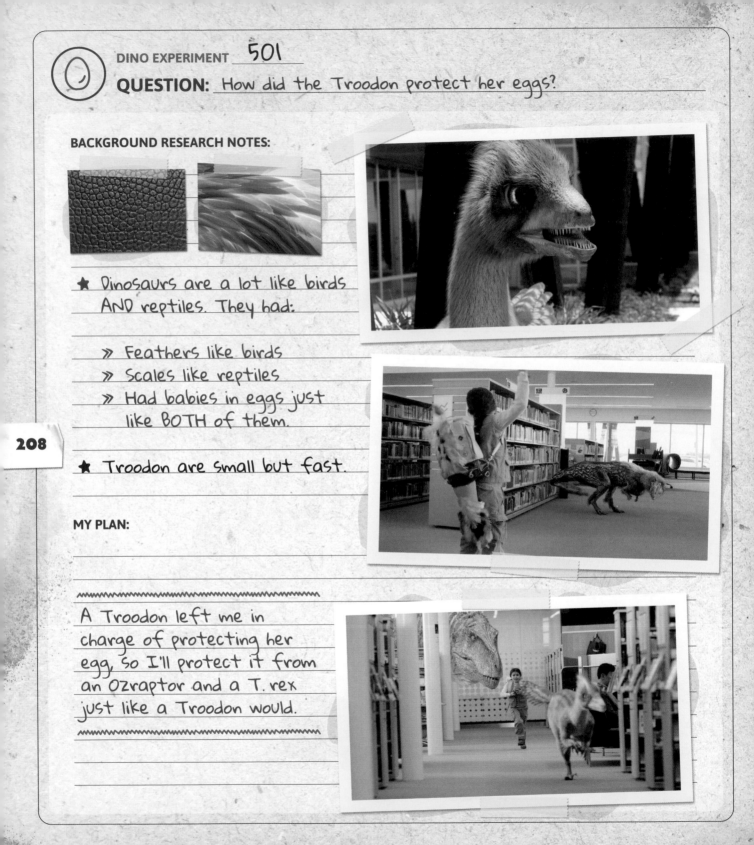

★ Dinosaurs are a lot like birds
AND reptiles. They had:

  » Feathers like birds
  » Scales like reptiles
  » Had babies in eggs just
     like BOTH of them.

★ Troodon are small but fast.

MY PLAN:

A Troodon left me in
charge of protecting her
egg, so I'll protect it from
an Ozraptor and a T. rex
just like a Troodon would.

FIELD NOTES:

1. I'm a Troodon today so I'm protecting the mama Troodon's egg but now an Ozraptor is trying to steal it!
   » Dinosaurs are like birds, so I'll do what birds do to protect their eggs—squawk loudly and flap my arms! It worked!

2. Oh no, now the egg is starting to hatch and a hungry T. rex is coming!
   » Dinosaurs are also like reptiles who put eggs in their mouths to carry them away from danger! I'll take the egg with me and run away! Phew, we got away!

3. Except the baby hatched and now the T. rex found us! Uh oh!
   » Update = The mom Troodon came back and is trying to get us to a herd of dinosaurs. We used our Troodon speed to get past the T. rex and into the herd—safety in numbers!

FINDING:

Troodons protect their eggs like reptiles AND birds.

★ They made loud noises to scare off smaller dinosaurs (like birds do!)
★ They moved their eggs to keep them safe from larger dinos (like reptiles do!)
★ They stayed in herds for safety

TYRANNOSAURUS REX

(Tie-ran-oh-sore-us)
Means "Tyrant Lizard King"

210

ROAR!

252 Million

201 Million

145 Million

TRIASSIC

JURASSIC

Lived in Western USA, Alberta and Saskatchewan, Canada

WHEN T. REX LIVED

US

CRETACEOUS		PALEOGENE	NEOGENE	QUATERNARY
	66 Million		23 Million	2.6 Million

TYRANNOSAURUS REX

Skull got stronger as it grew up.

MASSIVE JAW to deliver a SUPER STRONG BITE!! Could bite through BONE!

Sixty big teeth-described as "lethal bananas."

T. rex cousins had feathers, so the T. rex might have had feathers too!

Paleontologists are still trying to figure this out!

★ Weighed more than 20 bears.

★ Was longer than a firetruck

Had stereoscopic vision.
That means it could see in 3D!

Saara made this

Very good sense of smell.

One of the biggest predators to have ever lived on land.

Me vs. T. rex

Main prey were Triceratops and Edmontosaurus.

QUESTION: _Were T. rexes warm-blooded or cold-blooded?_

BACKGROUND RESEARCH NOTES:

★ Warm-blooded animals (like us!) make their own body heat. That means, whether it's warm or cold outside, their body temperature stays the same.

★ Cold-blooded animals get their body heat from their environment. So if it's hot outside, their body temperature is warmer, but if it's cold outside their body temp is colder.

WARM-BLOODED

COLD-BLOODED

214

MY PLAN:

To find out if T. rexes were cold-blooded or warm-blooded, I need to find a way to take their temperature inside where it is warm and outside where it is cold—good thing it's snowing today!

FIELD NOTES:

1. First I need to use my thermometer to take the T. rex's temperature when she's outside!
   » Update = It's 98.6 degrees Fahrenheit/37 degrees Celsius.

2. Now I need to lure the T. rex inside to take her temperature. I'll use chicken to get her inside.
   » Update = Mama T. rex was WAY too big to get inside, but her baby came in! Her temperature was ALSO 98.6 degrees Fahrenheit/ 37 degrees Celsius.

FINDING:

T. rexes are warm-blooded because their body temperature is the SAME inside and outside! This means they can control their own body temperature like humans!

WINS!

UGRUNAALUK

ORNITHISCHIA

(Oo-grew-nah-luk)
Means "Ancient Grazer"

216

252 Million

201 Million

145 Million

TRIASSIC

JURASSIC

UGRUNAALUK

★ Three times the weight of a polar bear, but only a little taller than me.

Name comes from the Alaskan Inupiat language.

Lived in cooler temperatures than many other dinosaurs.

BUT their climate was different then, so it wasn't as cold as it is now. ⟵ <u>Climate</u> means what the weather is like in an area.

During the summer, they lived in around-the-clock daylight, but the winters were VERY dark!

Known from lots of bones from a single bonebed.

That means lots of them were found together!

Me vs. Ugrunaaluk

Mostly known from fossils of teenage Ugrunaaluk.

DINO EXPERIMENT 608

QUESTION: How did dinosaurs survive the winter?

BACKGROUND RESEARCH NOTES:

Scavenging means eating food that another animal already hunted and left behind.

It's harder to hunt in the winter because a lot of animals hibernate when it's cold.

MY PLAN:

Dad says it's called a decoy!

Build a fake dead Triceratops in the snow and put hot dogs on it to attract predators!

FIELD NOTES:

1. The Troodon found my Triceratops decoy and is eating the hot dogs! That means some dinosaurs scavenged in the winter!

2. Now a herbivore called the Ugrunaaluk is approaching! She looks like she's also eating the hot dogs from my decoy! Did herbivores become carnivores in the winter?!

   » Update = Wrong! She wasn't eating the hot dogs, she was digging below the snow to find the grass underneath. Smart Ugrunaaluk!

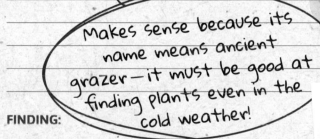

Makes sense because its name means ancient grazer—it must be good at finding plants even in the cold weather!

FINDING:

During the winter, some dinosaurs found food by scavenging and some found food by digging for it!

221

ZUUL

Defended itself by hitting predators with its massive and heavy tail club.

Armor on its back was as thick as a brick.

Zuul even had armor over her eyelids!

There is only one Zuul skeleton that exists, BUT it is one of the best-preserved dinosaurs!

It includes preserved DINO SKIN!

★ Just a little taller than my seestor Saara.

★ Weighed as much as 55 Saaras!

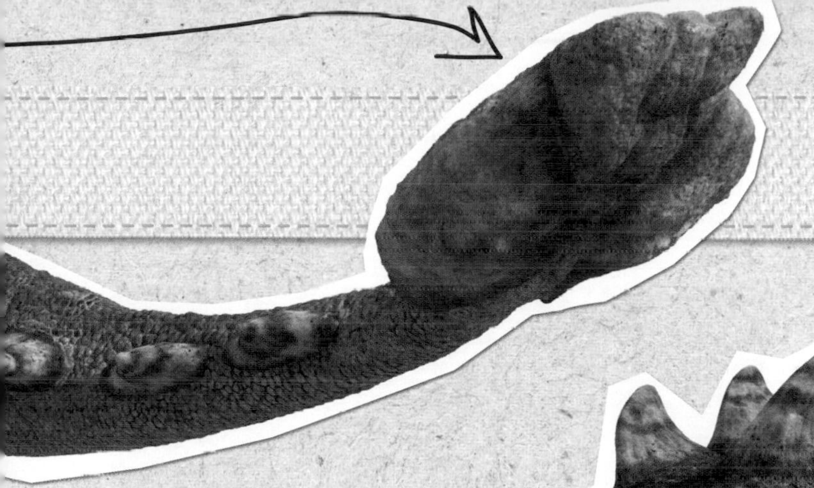

Zuul had a ton of armor! It had huge spikes on its tail and sides along with as many as 80,000 tiny pebbles (called ossicles) that acted like chainmail!

Like this! →

225

Zuul was NOT a fast moving dino! Moved as fast as a slow walking cow!

Me vs. Zuul...

But Zuul didn't need to be fast because it didn't have to chase its food, and it was ATTACK PROOF!

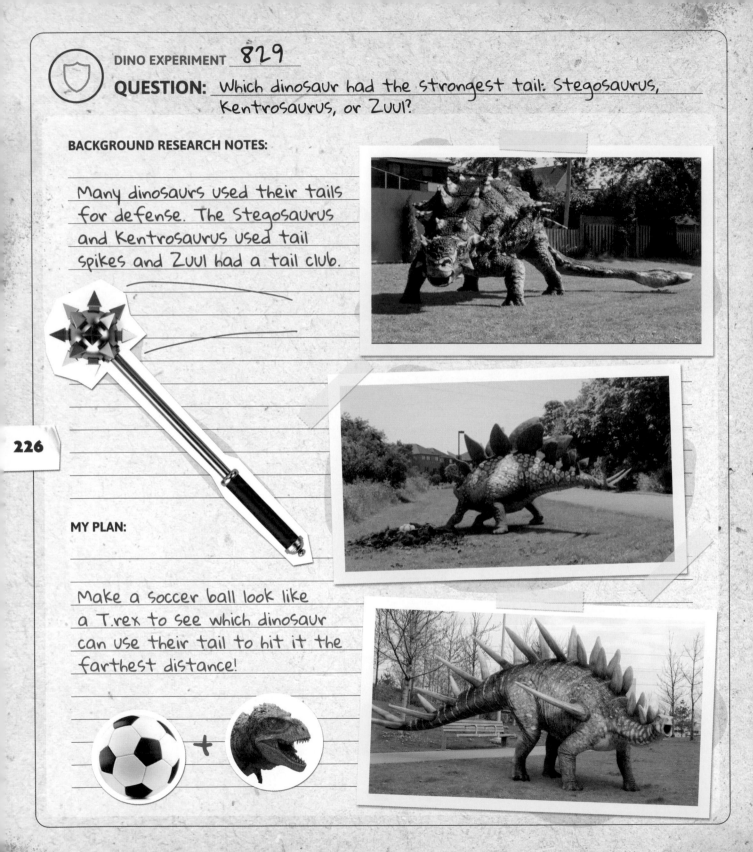

DINO EXPERIMENT __829__

QUESTION: Which dinosaur had the strongest tail: Stegosaurus, Kentrosaurus, or Zuul?

BACKGROUND RESEARCH NOTES:

Many dinosaurs used their tails for defense. The Stegosaurus and Kentrosaurus used tail spikes and Zuul had a tail club.

226

MY PLAN:

Make a soccer ball look like a T.rex to see which dinosaur can use their tail to hit it the farthest distance!

FIELD NOTES:

1. There's the Stegosaurus! She has a few spikes on her tail. I'm going to use my T. rex soccer ball to scare her. ROAR!
   » Update = The Stego sent the T. rex halfway across the soccer field. Pretty far!

2. Next up, the Kentrosaurus! He has the <u>SPIKIEST</u> tail of all the dinos. Let's see what happens when I surprise him with my T. rex soccer ball.
   » Update = The Kentro also only sent the ball halfway across the soccer field.

3. Finally, it's time for Zuul who doesn't have any spikes but has a massive tail club that weighs as much as my Dad!
   » Update = Nothing but net! Zuul's tail swing sent the T. rex soccer ball <u>ALL THE WAY ACROSS THE FIELD</u> and even scored a goal.

FINDING:

Zuul has the strongest tail. Tail club for the win.

ABOUT THE AUTHORS

My friends helped me write this guide. ← *J.J., Christin and Colleen!*

J.J. JOHNSON

J.J. is a multi-Emmy award winning executive producer, director, writer, and the creator of *Dino Dan, Dino Dan: Trek's Adventures* and *Dino Dana*. His favourite dinosaur was the T. rex but is now the Therizinosaurus.

← *Because of their super long claws*

CHRISTIN SIMMS

Christin is an Emmy award winning executive producer and writer on all three Dino series. Her favourite dinosaur has always been the Triceratops. ←

→ *They're best friends!*

Because its horns look cool ←

COLLEEN RUSSO JOHNSON, PHD ← *Dr. Colleen!*

Colleen is the director of research at Sinking Ship Entertainment which means she figures out ways to make things fun and educational. Her favourite dinosaur is the baby T. rex.

They're married! And like dinosaurs so much they named one of their kids "Rex"!

Just like Toby!

Here are some photos of us!

Mango Publishing, established in 2014, publishes an eclectic list of books by diverse authors—both new and established voices—on topics ranging from business, personal growth, women's empowerment, LGBTQ studies, health, and spirituality to history, popular culture, time management, decluttering, lifestyle, mental wellness, aging, and sustainable living. We were recently named 2019's #1 fastest growing independent publisher by Publishers Weekly. Our success is driven by our main goal, which is to publish high quality books that will entertain readers as well as make a positive difference in their lives.

Our readers are our most important resource; we value your input, suggestions, and ideas. We'd love to hear from you—after all, we are publishing books for you!

Please stay in touch with us and follow us at:

Facebook: Mango Publishing

Twitter: @MangoPublishing

Instagram: @MangoPublishing

LinkedIn: Mango Publishing

Pinterest: Mango Publishing

Sign up for our newsletter at www.mangopublishinggroup.com and receive a free book!

Join us on Mango's journey to reinvent publishing, one book at a time.